Rose Water & Orange Blossoms

FRESH AND CLASSIC RECIPES FROM MY LEBANESE KITCHEN

BY MAUREEN ABOOD

PHOTOGRAPHY BY JASON VARNEY

Running Press
PHILADELPHIA · LONDON

Published by Running Press,
A Member of the Perseus Books Group

Books published by Running Press are available at special discounts for bulk purchases in the United
States by corporations, institutions, and other organizations. For more information, please contact
the Special Markets Department at the Perseus Books Group, 2300 Chestnut Street, Suite 200,
Philadelphia, PA 19103, or call (800) 810-4145, ext. 5000, or e-mail special.markets@perseusbooks.com.

ISBN 978-0-7624-5486-0

Library of Congress Control Number: 2014952836

E-book ISBN 978-0-7624-5604-8

9   8   7   6   5   4   3   2   1
Digit on the right indicates the number of this printing

Designed by Joshua McDonnell
Edited by Kristen Green Wiewora
Hand-lettering and Illustrations by Katie Hatz
Food Styling by Chris Lanier
Prop Styling by Paige Hicks
Typography: Avenir, Constantia, and Gonte

Page 14 photo courtesy of Maureen Abood. Page 19 photo © Stephanie N. Baker.

Running Press Book Publishers
2300 Chestnut Street
Philadelphia, PA 19103-4371

Visit us on the web!
www.offthemenublog.com

For my parents, Maryalice and Camille Abood, and in memory of all of my grandparents. You've taught me the most important ingredient in the Lebanese kitchen: love.

And for my husband, Dan Shaheen. I'm so blessed to share a Lebanese kitchen and home with you.

Introduction

"And when you crush an apple with your teeth, say to it in your heart,
'Your seeds shall live in my body,
And the buds of your tomorrow shall blossom in my heart,
And your fragrance shall be my breath,
And together we shall rejoice through all the seasons.'"

—Khalil Gibran

"Have you ever been to Lebanon?"

It's a question I've been asked all my life, by kind and interested people, especially when I mention my Lebanese family, my passion for Lebanese cooking, and my desire to write about it too.

My answer, until recently, was simple: Nope. I hadn't visited Lebanon, and it pained me. It pained me not only because I hoped that this lack didn't somehow make my Lebanese-ness less . . . authentic? . . . but also, and above all, because I pined, almost bitterly now, for this place that had loomed so large in my imagination all of my life.

I have tried to piece together the stories of my grandparents, all but one of them gone well before I was ten years old. I have tracked down every aunt and uncle who would bear with me to interview them, plied with luncheon and cake, about any detail they could remember of the younger lives of my grandparents: their childhoods in mountainous and verdant Lebanese villages, their marriages (arranged: I was, and remain, fascinated), the arduous journeys they made a century ago to start new lives in the United States, and their infrequent return visits back home, where the ravages of war would hold them, and all of us, at arm's length.

Their stories have been so well constructed in my mind that there are times when I have wondered what's fact and what's fiction. I wondered too, then, when at last I visited Lebanon for the first time a few years ago, if I'd built it up so much that the trip couldn't possibly live up to all that I'd hoped for. Packing to leave, I considered calling it off just to avoid a possible letdown.

Good thing that was a fleeting thought. Lebanon welcomed me with a generosity akin to the most lavish table one could set. There were cousins and aunts and uncles I'd never met, but whose faces and embraces were familiar with family feel. There was meaning around every corner, in the architecture and the terrain, the sea and the sky. And in the cedar trees, which lined the courtyard of the moody monastery of Lebanese Saint Charbel. Now the cedars of Lebanon became living, animated beauties for me, and not just an impression carved in the gold charms so many of us wear.

The food I experienced in Lebanon was both

exactly what I had imagined, and beyond what I could have imagined. In the home of my cousin May in Beirut, there was a dazzling spread—one that she crafted on a day's notice: kibbeh nayeh (yes, I ate it raw more than once in Lebanon; it was spicy and delicious), kofta with toum garlic sauce, silky smooth hummus, thick labneh, and a massive platter of grape leaves rolled from leaves she had foraged in our family's village, Dier Mimas in the south. She made 300 pinkie-sized stuffed grape leaves (the smaller they are, the more difficult to roll). Also, platters tall with green plums and kumquats. There were copious Lebanese wines and *arak*, our strong anise liqueur. Then desserts of all sorts filled the table, but even my sweet tooth couldn't help

being dazzled just as much by the fresh fava beans; handed to each one at the table straight from a brown bag from the farmers' market. We plucked them from their pods, popped the beans from their thick green skins, salted them, and ate. It was the finest palate cleanser I've ever tasted.

My trip to Lebanon was so rich with inspiration that I'm still, in a sense, unpacking. Perhaps those sorts of experiences, like the finest meals, are meant to be savored and digested slowly, thoughtfully, and gratefully.

Fig and Anise Jam with Walnuts, page 216

The path to this book has been not unlike the path that led me to Lebanon. It's been on my mind for such a long time that I hardly recall a time when I wasn't thinking of writing about Lebanese recipes, and the stories that are their finest ingredients.

I was always keenly aware of my ethnicity as a Lebanese American; this was most distinctly expressed in the kitchen and at the table. Neighborhood kids who were lucky enough to be at our house on a day when my grandmother on my dad's side—my Sitto—and my mother were baking always received a warm rolled-up flatbread, which we called Syrian bread, slathered with melting butter and dusted with salt. Those days resulted in pans piled high with savory pies filled with spinach or meat, loaves of soft, chewy breads topped with oily za'atar, then sugared fried dough as the end-of-day treat.

You can see why I made it a point to wake up early with Sitto to sit on the counter and watch her mix the dough in a huge blue-speckled roasting pan. She encouraged me to poke my hesitant hand in the gooey mass of flour and water, whispering, *"Feel that dough, how good it feels,"* a secret whose breath lingered in my ear long after she was gone.

And why, when I was in graduate school laboring over English literature, my weekly break was to visit Sitto in her delicious little apartment. She'd buzz me in with a buzz that would sound out far longer than it took to open the door and walk up the stairs to where she was standing, in her housedress (I never saw her in a pair of pants), wearing lipstick, and with neatly combed snow white hair, waiting for me.

What went on during those respite hours from study was baking, of course, and other cooking (she taught me an oregano chicken with garlic I'll never forget), all of it woven like her intricately crocheted table runners into a long, uninterrupted conversation. Sitto loved to tease and laugh and poke fun. She'd nod to me as I scored and cut through her crisp, fragrant baklawa with a knife so dull it must have never been sharpened (but was used so much she never put it away, leaning it on the side of the sink instead), and tsk me into toughening my hands to pull charred eggplant for baba gannouj from the oven bare.

Sitto reached in there with adept fingers that met no heat they couldn't take, and got her well-chosen (firm, not too big) eggplant going. She flipped it barehanded; she pulled it out with bare hands, and sort of threw it onto the kitchen counter as if to say: *"Take that, you hot smoky eggplant. I am Sitto, and I am in charge."*

This Sitto-strength, in a phrase, is what I aspire to every day.

My mother runs her kitchen in other, equally influential, ways. Here is where my three brothers, my sister, and I learn (it's ongoing) the art of Lebanese hospitality, of welcome that is so important to us. For my dad, that was epitomized by the use of a fresh, white tablecloth on the table. This to him was the best way one could eat a meal in his own home. Whether any of us were ever to take up cooking, or baking, was of little importance to my mother or my father. More so was the ability, the cultivated skill, the fundamental generosity to put anyone who crosses your threshold in a state of complete ease, with the feeling they really don't want to leave any time soon.

The desire to make good food, though, was instilled in each of us. There were Lebanese and American feasts on our table most every night of the year, platters of our favorite buttery

Baalbek ruins, Lebanon

I have of my father in the final days of his life was his desire to be together with his family at the table. He was no longer eating, because of the ravages of his terminal cancer, which took his life only weeks after his diagnosis. But he sat with us anyway for a few brief moments, a full plate of my mother's Lebanese food in front of him. His mantra to us had always been: Never let anyone sit at the table alone. And if many of you can gather, do it.

~~~~

chicken and hushweh rice, Mom's big crisp romaine salads with lemon and oil, cabbage rolls and kibbehs and green bean stew ladled hot from the stove over fragrant cinnamon rice. And, often, desserts, my mother's favorite part of a meal (and now mine, too), everything from creamy rice pudding to cakes and cookies of all kinds. Big bowls of ripe fruit were a given. And her simple, but always adored, little plate of chocolates, her own homey version of mignardises, something I've come to include no matter what I'm serving for dessert.

These were meals my mother could have easily and no doubt with less headache pulled off single-handedly—but didn't, preferring instead the opportunity to get her children at any age together and involved in the kitchen. When friends, especially parents working hard to raise close-knit children, wonder how my parents raised their five so well, I think especially of those times in the kitchen, where we have always and often found ourselves together. Among the many abiding memories

My milestone trip to Lebanon was just one of a few important stepping stones on the path to my life as a food blogger and writing this book. When I went to culinary school a few years ago, I wanted to make a change in my life as much as I wanted to cook great food. I left the job I'd been working in Chicago for years, left the neighborhood where I'd been living all those years too, and headed west to San Francisco.

Growing up in a big Lebanese family is wonderful, but it doesn't always leave room for much solo time—time to hike the inroads that tell us who we are, which can only be walked alone. Even when I went away to college at Saint Mary's, Notre Dame, I had my brothers and sister there: special times I wouldn't trade. But perhaps not eking out enough solo time, over time, played its role in keeping me at arm's length from the things I did, and wanted to do, best. Maybe that also played its role in leading up to a painfully brief marriage I entered, and exited, not long before the seeds of change (we're talking watermelon-sized seeds, not mustard) started sprouting deep within.

Thankfully even as I embraced an independence that allowed me to explore my future in new and exciting ways, the closeness of my family continued to be a blessing in encouraging me on the path. At a crucial point, during a difficult period, my sister, Peggy, gifted me with a candy-making class at the French Pastry School in Chicago, a precursor to my culinary school leap. That week in the kitchen taught me about tempering chocolate, respecting the ingredients, and listening closely to what the process is telling you. In learning to make candy, I found the perfect metaphor for what was happening in my life, learning to temper, respect, and listen . . . to myself. And what I heard when I listened closely was a call to the kitchen, and not just for a weekend or a week, but to head in full-on and full-time.

From the first day I walked through the doors of Tante Marie's Cooking School, hiking the lovely, challenging hills of San Francisco to get there, I started having fun with what I do. My uniform of black-checked pants and chef's coat with my happy green Dansko clogs gave me the sweet pleasure that only a uniform worn for work one loves can give: *I'm becoming a chef!* I thought, every time I donned my whites. Of course, I had that same thought, but without the smile, without the exclamation point, every time I sliced into my fingers, burned the caramel, or had to clean out the compost bins. But even then, I took the knocks and found there was nothing, nothing at all, that could detract from the joy of working hard at something one loves to do.

Culinary school is in large measure about learning to cook without recipes, without going back to a guide to help carry the load and figure out the next step. Our Sherpa, once we got the hang of it and could really let go, would be our own selves.

We learned to fly solo in the kitchen just as I was learning to do in all aspects of my life: by tuning in to our senses—taste and sound and smell and touch—to show us what to do next, how to correct course when necessary, and how to end with a good result, no matter what happened on the way there.

≈≈≈

The solo flight west to culinary school left me with a question that I knew only I could answer: what to do next. Writing and diving deep into Lebanese cuisine by launching my blog, Rose Water & Orange Blossoms, was my goal, but where to do that kind of work without taking another full-time job that would drain me of my time and appetite for it? Heading back home to Michigan, to northern Michigan in Harbor Springs—"Up North"—where my family had spent so much of our life, came into focus. I'd live in the family cottage there, freelance, spend plenty of time in the solitude a writer craves, and see what happens.

I had thought often of how one experiences a marked increase in appetite upon entering Harbor Springs. This is because of Up North terroir—terroir being a "sense of place," and how the environment from which anything is grown imparts a unique quality that is specific to that region. The terroir in Harbor Springs begins with the water: The ultra-cold, natural springs that bubble out of the beaches and the drinking fountains are like fountains of youth, a Holy Grail. One could not taste purer, sweeter water anywhere. This purity extends to the light here, yellow light that casts itself across the summer days, and the violet veil that it becomes at dusk and dawn. It's an orchestration, along with soil, bay breezes, and other exquisite secrets of the seasons that only a higher power, God, could conduct. The outcome in food is an explosion of flavor, color, and texture, grand and fleeting like the fireworks finale over the bay on the fourth of July. They *boom* and strike awe in us; they echo down the lake. Then they are gone until next year.

So when I left northern California, a place that is known for its terroir, I wondered where I could go next that measured up. I knew that I would not be seeking a position on the line in a restaurant, but rather would want to find a quiet place where I could settle in, cook, and write. Ideally this creative life would take place near a body of water (right?!).

I left my things in storage, and headed north. It became clear to me that terroir doesn't just impact foodstuffs. Terroir produces . . . us. We are products of our familial upbringings, and products of place. The same environmental elements that make the tomatoes at Coveyou Scenic Farms so perfect or the local honey at Pond Hill so divine are having their effect on us, too.

~~~~~

Summers on the porch Up North have always brought visitors by. From the start, my dad would wave them on up to join him on the white wicker chairs for a visit. Before they could hit the top step, he was turning to his daughters to bring out glasses of iced lemonade for everyone.

On Dan Shaheen's first visit to our place on Main Street, he'd come over from Charlevoix on the water in a big, bad cigarette boat with his brothers. I've always thought that boat was yellow, but Dan says no, red. They were very young, swarthy men; no doubt they sauntered through town and hung out on the docks looking at the pretty girls pass by. They didn't leave, though, without visiting my dad, Camille. Since their own dad died unexpectedly, a young man himself just a few years before, my father had stood close by the boys and their mom and their sisters as they put their lives and their auto dealership back together in the difficult aftermath, and then for years beyond that. In other words: They were close friends. Close Lebanese friends—which means, you know, that they were cousins.

The brothers came up on the porch, my dad waving them over and turning to his daughters for the lemonade. Dan says it was a glass of pink lemonade that I handed him, and that I had long brown braids on either side of my 12-year-old face. He must have pulled on one of the braids and cast a certain spell, one that said: I'll be seeing you back here somewhere down the line, and then for good.

For a lot of years (read: thirty) after that, my Aunt Hilda, Dad's sister, was the epicenter for Dan and me to hear, however sidelined, how the other one was doing. She and I would sit at her kitchen table and she'd fill me in on what was happening with everybody we knew, from cousins to more cousins to the Shaheens (Danny is a *hanoun*, she'd say, like you) and the family over in Lebanon.

Hilda's best friend? Dan's mama, Louise. They shared the same towns (Flint, then Lansing), ran with all the same people, had both lost their

husbands too young, and were "like that"—two fingers crossed: tight. Sisters. Cousins. Close friends (my own mom was of course part of that circle of Lebanese lovin' ladies too).

Right around the time that my sister-in-law passed away far too young in 2009, Dan and I were in a similar state of mind. The road had been bumpy. The Path of Life had not, in many ways, been what either of us had in mind. At the funeral, I stood up and sang a tear-laden Ave Maria and Dan says he sat in his pew listening, watching, and wondering. He came up to say hello after.

A year or so later when I was in San Francisco, Aunt Hilda had gotten very sick, to the end-time, and I came back to Michigan. We were for a good week up at the hospital holding the vigil.

At Hilda's wake, the room was jammed with all of the Lebanese dressed in their handsome black, laughing and crying and laughing some more.

I was telling Aunt Rita that I was moving back to Michigan after culinary school, when I turned to see the handsomest of them all, Dan Shaheen, standing by my side. It was our first real, head-on conversation since the lemonade-visit when I was a kid.

We nodded about Aunt Hilda (she always told him he was her favorite, and he was genuinely surprised to hear she'd said the same to me, and others…), but then he cut to the chase: *You're coming back? When?* I told him I'd be heading directly Up North, where I'd stay.

See you on the porch for a glass of lemonade, he said.

And that we did. Happily ever after.

~~~~~

Rose Water & Orange Blossoms comes to you from these stories, and of course, so many more. Here you will find classic Lebanese recipes, the ones our parents and grandparents cooked for us with the kind of love that is their hallmark—but that often were never written down, or got lost in the shuffle of life. I also offer recipes that are inspired by our ingredients and our style of cooking, to make something fresh and delightfully new.

All of my recipes emphasize spices, fruits and vegetables, lean meats, grains, and lots of fresh herbs. I am influenced by the seasons, cooking with what is freshest at the farmers' market and making use of the robust Lebanese tradition of canning and preserving.

The book is laden with the lushness of ingredients like spearmint and floral waters, sumac and cinnamon, pomegranates and pistachios, succulent lamb, bulgur wheat, and lentils.

Perhaps you will find here a bridge to the foods you have known and want to cook for yourself or your family. It is my hope that this book will inspire you to remember, and to savor with pride, your own Lebanese family tree. Or perhaps you are one of the many who loves the flavors and ingredients of the Middle East, or are new to Lebanese cuisine, or have been served these dishes in the home of your Lebanese neighbors or friends. I hope that what you find here opens the door to a kitchen where you feel right at home with warmth and welcome, and don't want to leave any time soon.

You're Invited!

You have a standing invitation to join me in my kitchen to see how many of the dishes in this book are prepared. Wondering how to roll a grape leaf, form a fatayar, or open a pomegranate? Nothing beats seeing the methods in action. Join me at www.maureenabood.com for personal video demonstrations of the following recipes and more:

- How to make ultra-smooth hummus

- How to form fatayar and sfeha pies

- How to roll grape leaves

- How to core koosa

- How to open a pomegranate

- How to cut baklawa diamonds

- How to mold ma'moul butter cookies

and many more!

NOTES ABOUT SPECIAL INGREDIENTS

Bulgur (also known as *burghul*), not to be confused with cracked wheat, is par-cooked, dried cracked wheat. It can be softened simply by soaking it in water, or cooked like rice and other grains. Bulgur is available in varying grades of coarseness, from #1 fine grade through #4 coarse grade.

Dry Skinned Chickpeas are a game-changer! These par-cooked, dry chickpeas have already been skinned, which saves lots of time with recipes that call for chickpeas without their tough skins, and need only to be cooked for about 2 hours. There is no substitute for skinned chickpeas when it comes to the best-tasting, smoothest hummus (page 49).

Fava Beans are wonderful fresh, but we use them mostly in their dried, and often then cooked, form. Look for dried favas that do not have skins; they are big, plump, and creamy white.

Knafeh Dough is very finely shredded phyllo dough. *Knafeh* (pronounced kuh-NAF-ee) dough is typically called *kataifi* (pronounced kuh-TIE-fee) dough, the Greek iteration of knafeh. The shredded dough is used to make all kinds of Lebanese pastry, typically of the buttery, syrupy sort.

Mahleb, the kernel in the pit of the specially cultivated St. Lucie or mahaleb cherry, is called for in many Lebanese baked goods and is found in recipes from across the Levant as *mahlab*, *mahaleb*, *mahleppi*, and *mahlebi*. The cherries themselves are so delicious that I suppose it's not so shocking that someone, somewhere deep in the past, kept eating right past the flesh and crunched away at the pit. There that adventurous eater discovered an almond-like flavor, a flavor reminiscent of the cherry but not precisely cherry, with a certain bitterness to boot. For the most aromatic flavor, grind only as much mahleb as you need just before using it, and store the rest of the whole kernels in the freezer, where they'll stay nice for a year or longer.

Orange Blossom Water and Rose Water are floral distillations from the flowers' petals. Clearly, I love them very much! And I am not alone. Our recipes (and dare I say, our lives?) would not be the same without their delicate presence.

Pistachio and Walnut Oils are the essence of the nuts that are so important to Lebanese culture and cuisine. These wonderful oils can be used to dress vegetables, salads, or as a dipping oil. Their freshness is crucial; throw away any with the slightest hint of rancidity.

Pomegranate Molasses is simply pomegranate juice reduced to a syrup. Its flavor is tangy and sweet, and it is widely available. You can make your own by boiling down pomegranate juice until it is just thick enough to coat the back of a spoon (don't boil it longer, as it will thicken a bit while cooling off).

Sumac Powder is made from pulverized dried sumac berries, a spice that has been ramping up Middle Eastern dishes since the beginning of time. *Sumac* (pronounced *SOO-mahk*) is an ancient spice, with a flavor that is tangy, lemony, and bright—not surprising, given its beautiful bright red hue.

Za'atar is a spice blend of dried wild thyme, sesame seeds, and sumac. Some versions include salt as well, so taste yours before adding salt when you're cooking with za'atar.

Tahini is a paste of ground sesame seeds, traditionally used to make dips and sauces as well as sesame sweets. I like to think of tahini as grown-up peanut butter, but thinner. Tahini oil separates from the seed paste over time, so it must be stirred well before using. The shelf-life of tahini is long (when refrigerated), but the paste at the bottom of the tahini container tends to harden over time, so buying it fresh every few months is best. The richness of tahini is of the sort that is good for us, with healthy omegas and high protein. Two types of tahini are available: darker tahini from toasted sesame seeds, and blonde tahini from raw seeds. Since I'm a fan of anything toasted, I prefer the deep golden brown, nutty, all-natural tahini. Cans of Joyva brand tahini and white containers of Lebanese imported Alkanater Tahini Extra are on my A-list.

See pages 242 to 243 for sources for special ingredients.

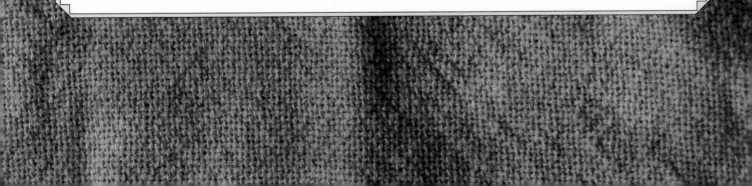

THE WAY WITH LABAN

When I've envisioned the story of my grandmother Nabeha's arranged marriage in Lebanon, and her immediate, teary-eyed departure to the United States with her new husband, one of the more lighthearted among the many serious thoughts I've had about her journey is that she may have carried with her the makings for laban. *Laban*, which is simply yogurt, is on the table in some form or another as a savory accompaniment for most every Lebanese meal (breakfast, lunch, dinner) and it's made using a culture—a starter, or *rawbeh* (RAU-bee)—from the last batch of yogurt.

When Nabeha started up her own kitchen in Michigan after leaving Lebanon so many years ago, I like to believe the story that she brought some of her mother's rawbeh with her so that she could make good laban here. It may well have survived the boat ride over without much refrigeration, and it would have given her comfort in the connection it gave her to Lebanon, to her mother, to the life she left behind as a girl of seventeen. The story goes that she didn't want the marriage, didn't want to go to the United States, and didn't want to leave the boy she was in love with in Lebanon behind.

She cried rivers, but in the end entered the arrangement, got on a boat, and started a new life. I think of the laban as her safety blanket, her piece of home.

If Nabeha brought her mother's starter with her to make laban, and then if her daughters (let's face it, the men didn't make the laban) used starter from Nabeha's laban to get their own line of yogurt going, and then if I took some of the yogurt from these aunts of mine to get my yogurt going . . . well, you can see that it's possible for the laban to live as long as a family does, following the branches of the family tree as far as the tree is willing and able to grow.

Making my own laban is a ritual that signified for me perhaps the first step in creating my own Lebanese kitchen, one that was and continues to be imbued with a yearning toward the kitchens of my mother, my aunts, my grandmothers, and theirs before them. Like Nabeha setting sail to a new country, making my own laban started me on a journey to womanhood. In laban-making there is both an independence and a dependence, making something new by your own hand, yet something that doesn't begin without including the very best elements of what came before us, starting us on our way.

Laban (Homemade Yogurt)

Lebanese yogurt, *laban*, is one of those things we can make at home that is satisfying on so many levels. I make a batch of healthy, delicious yogurt nearly every week, and I never get over the little thrill of using a spoonful of the last batch to start the next one, or lifting the lid of my incubated milk to find that the yogurt set up beautifully. Plus, the economics of homemade yogurt are a kitchen cost-saver's dream. Special equipment, like the yogurt makers that became so popular years ago, isn't needed to make great yogurt. You can use a thermometer to gauge the temperature throughout the process, or, once you get the hang of it, go old-school as our Sittos did, and let your knowing finger be the judge. Find more tips for making great homemade yogurt on page 28.

Makes about 8 cups / 2 kg

½ gallon / 2 L whole milk

2 tablespoons plain, unsweetened yogurt

Rinse a large heavy pot (3-quart / 3 L or larger) with cool water. Every Lebanese woman I know does this to help prevent scorching; I don't question it. Add the milk, and if you're using a thermometer, clip it to the side of the pan without letting it touch the bottom. Heat the milk slowly over medium-low heat to just below a boil (210°F / 98°C), about 30 minutes, depending on how cold the milk is to start. Heating the milk too quickly can result in grainy yogurt. Stay nearby, because the milk will froth up, and as it begins to boil it will rise swiftly in the pan and can overflow. Move the pot off of the heat immediately when it hits 210°F / 98°C, or when the milk froths and starts to rise.

Let the milk cool down to 110°F to 115°F / 43°C to 46°C, stirring occasionally. If you are not using a thermometer, the equivalent is when your pinkie can just withstand being swirled in the milk for ten seconds before you have to pull it away. Arriving at this temperature can take an hour. To speed it up, place the pot in an ice bath in the sink, stirring the milk regularly to release the heat.

Temper and loosen the starter by stirring some of the warm milk into it, a tablespoon at a time, about 6 tablespoons total. Stir the warmed starter yogurt thoroughly into the milk. You will notice a skin formed on the surface of the milk while it was heating up; that can be stirred right in with the starter.

Remove the thermometer if you've used one, and cover the pot with its lid. Drape a clean kitchen towel over the pot and set it aside, undisturbed, in a warm spot up to 110°F / 43°C for 6 to 12 hours. The longer the yogurt incubates, the more developed the flavor will be. I like to make yogurt in the evening and let it rest overnight and well into the next day. An ideal incubator is the oven, turned off (the oven can be heated on the lowest setting for a minute before placing the pan in, just to encourage warmth, but don't forget to turn it off!).

Remove the lid from the pot. The milk will have thickened into yogurt, which you can tell by lightly jiggling the pot. Chill the pot of yogurt, undisturbed as of yet, for a day or so before eating it or straining to thicken it for labneh.

~~~~~~~~~~

Note: If the milk cools below 110°F / 43°C (or your pinkie can stand it longer than ten seconds) before you introduce the starter, slowly warm the milk up again to 110 to 115°F / 43°C to 46°C. If in this process of reheating, the temperature goes above 115°F / 46°C, wait again until it comes back down to 110°F to 115°F / 43°C to 46°C.

Everything You Need to Know to Make Good Yogurt

The milk. I always use local organic milk, grass-fed when available, because I want anything I eat that much of to be as clean and healthy as possible. Yogurt can be made with skim, 1 percent, 2 percent, or whole milk. Lower fat milk yields a less flavorful, somewhat thinner yogurt. You can add powdered milk before boiling the milk to get a thicker result when using lower fat milk—⅓ cup / 80 mL for ½ gallon / 2 L of milk. Whole milk is the best you can use for both good flavor and thick texture. I've even taken a page out of Aunt Hilda's playbook and poured in a pint / ½ L of heavy cream with my milk (no need to adjust the amount of starter when you do this). As you can imagine, the cream makes a rich yogurt that is like the luxe wedding gown of all laban—lavish, special-occasion loveliness.

The starter. Yogurt is made like sourdough, with a starter from your last batch. If you have no last batch, get some from a yogurt-making friend, or use store-bought yogurt. Much of your yogurt-making success depends upon the starter, the rawbeh. If you buy commercial yogurt for your starter, be sure it's plain, unflavored, and unsweetened. I use whole milk rawbeh, even if I'm making a low-fat laban with low-fat milk.

The flavor. Yogurt is made with such simplicity, and so few ingredients, that it is going to taste only as good as your ingredients. The Lebanese enjoy their yogurt with a certain tang, a certain depth of flavor that is unlike the typical sweetened or bland plain commercial yogurt. When my homemade yogurt lacks depth of flavor, I salt it lightly and leave it out on the counter for the day, which brings up the flavor. A squeeze of lemon juice also nudges the yogurt's flavor along. Or I try to find a starter that has great flavor for my next batch, from someone else's laban or from the homemade laban that can be purchased at many Middle Eastern markets. Authentic Lebanese laban is often made with goat's milk, which, like goat cheese, is softly complex and rich. Try using goat's milk yogurt as a starter for yogurt made with cow's milk, a nice balance of flavors.

The Whole Cloth: Straining Laban for Labneh

When I ironed stacks of my father's handkerchiefs when I was a young girl, I knew that at least one of them was going to be tucked away in the kitchen by my mother to strain her labneh and other fresh homemade cheeses (she just tried to avoid using his favorite ones, with his initials embroidered in silver thread in the corner). I realized at some point that my Sitto also used a white hankie, and that this must be the tradition of Lebanese cooks for the thin, clean drain they could get through the handkerchief cloth.

The straining process used to achieve the thick, rich texture of labneh or the even thicker labneh cheese preserved in oil can make use of a variety of different methods: fine-gauge cheesecloth works much better than standard, open-weave cheesecloth. If you have only the latter, double or triple it up. There are also specialty draining bags available for cheese and nut milk, and I have always found ink-free paper towel in a single layer lining a colander does the job nicely. If you happen to have someone in your life who still uses cotton hankies, use one and you'll be in good Lebanese company.

Labneh (Thick Yogurt)

A day without labneh in my kitchen feels like a day without sunshine. Labneh is one of those things that always seems to be on the table, in my refrigerator, on the stove, or draining in the sink. Labneh accompanies many savory Lebanese dishes, and is also excellent drizzled with honey, topped with granola, or mixed with crushed dried mint (page 31), fresh herbs, and scallions as a dip for crudité. I love labneh as much for the ways in which its thick creaminess enriches a plate, as for the ways in which making a batch enriches a day, and over time, a life.

Makes about 3 cups / 690 g

8 cups / 2 kg yogurt (laban), or 1 recipe of homemade yogurt (page 26)

½ teaspoon kosher salt

Place a large colander in the sink or over a bowl to catch the dripping whey, and line the colander with a large sheer hankie, fine cheesecloth, a specialty draining bag, or an ink-free paper towel (a single layer).

Pour the yogurt into the lined colander. To encourage and speed up the draining process, gravity is your friend. If you're using a large hankie or cheesecloth, tie together the opposite corners of the cloth, hobo-style, and hang it from the faucet (be sure you can do without running the water for several hours, ideally overnight) with the colander underneath to catch the bundle if it falls. Or hang the bundle from a long-handled wooden spoon suspended over a deep bowl or pot. If you're using paper towels, cover the top of the yogurt with another towel; keep the colander in the sink, or place it over a deep bowl (double boiler-style) to catch the whey. The whey can then be discarded.

Drain the yogurt at least 4 to 6 hours, preferably overnight. It does not need to be refrigerated while draining.

When the labneh is thickened, scrape it from the lining of the colander with a rubber spatula or, if it pulls away cleanly as it tends to do when drained in paper towel, simply turn the labneh out into a bowl. Add the salt and whisk the labneh well to smooth out any lumps. Aunt Hilda was so devoted to smoothing her labneh that she used to whip it in the stand mixer for a smoothness that would meet her exacting standards. A paper towel can be tucked in over the top of the labneh in an airtight container to absorb the excess whey.

Cover and chill the labneh, ideally overnight, before serving. It will keep in an airtight container in the refrigerator for a couple of weeks.

Toum (Garlic Sauce)

If there were ever a love song to garlic, Lebanese *toum* (pronounced TOOM) is the finest aria of them all. *Toum*, which means "garlic" in Arabic, is pure garlic flavor that is brightened with lemon; you'll find yourself stirring toum into just about any recipe that calls for minced garlic, as well as its classic Lebanese pairing with grilled meats (such as Yogurt Marinated Chicken Skewers, page 123). A spoonful of toum elevates any steamed or roasted vegetable, or pasta or grains—or as a dipping sauce for good bread. I've even taken to slathering it on my homemade white pizzas before baking. Making toum requires a slow and steady hand to emulsify the garlic and oil in the food processor; consider toum like an aïoli with no egg. There are many methods cooks use to avoid a broken toum emulsion, such as adding an egg white, cooked potato, or cornstarch to the mix. I like my toum made without any of those, which can be replaced with patience—and a little ice water, which helps the emulsion hold.

Makes about 2 cups / 420 g

1 head fresh garlic (squeeze it: it should be solid and very firm)

1 teaspoon kosher salt

Juice of 1 lemon

1¾ cups / 420 mL neutral oil, such as safflower or canola

4 to 6 tablespoons / 60 to 90 mL ice water

Peel the garlic cloves and slice them in half lengthwise. If there is a green germ in any of the cloves, remove it to prevent the bitter, burning flavor it imparts.

Process the garlic cloves with the salt in the food processor, stopping and scraping down the sides a few times, until the garlic is minced. Add the lemon juice and pulse several times to combine.

With the processor on, begin to drizzle the oil in so slowly that the stream turns to a dribble at times; use the oil drip hole in the top of the processor if yours has one. After ¼ cup / 60 mL of the oil has been added, slowly pour in a tablespoon / 15 mL of the ice water. Continue slowly drizzling in the oil and slowly adding a tablespoon of ice water after every ¼ cup / 60 mL of oil until the sauce is thickened and all of the oil has been incorporated. This takes about 7 minutes.

The sauce will be slightly thick, with some body, but still pourable. Store the toum in an airtight container in the refrigerator for several weeks.

Nana (Dried Mint)

Mint, or *nana* (pronounced NAH-nuh), is the hallmark herb of Lebanese recipes, ubiquitously imparting its fresh, bright flavor. Dried mint is often used together with fresh mint in Lebanese recipes for deeper mint flavor. It's simple to make yourself, and the crisp, dried leaves keep for months in an airtight container (I use a jar and leave it out on the counter). Always crush dried mint leaves between your palms right when you're ready to use it. The resulting bright and dark green mint dust is a go-to finishing touch, especially with salads and laban or labneh dishes. Note that the fresh mint must be just-plucked from its stem and bone dry before you begin, so that it will crisp up more readily in the drying process. When measuring, note that ¼ cup of whole dried leaves results in about a teaspoon of crushed dried mint.

Makes about 1 cup whole leaves / 3 grams dried mint

1 large bunch fresh mint sprigs

If possible, do not rinse the mint; just shake it off to clean it, so that it is as dry as possible. Pluck the leaves from their stems.

Dry the mint swiftly in the microwave, which yields the greenest dried mint. Working in batches, place the leaves in a single layer on a microwavable china plate lined with a paper towel, or on a paper plate. Dry the mint in 30-second intervals (about three, depending on your machine) until the leaves are curled and starting to dry, but still bright green (there may be some dark spots). The leaves will crisp up further once they have cooled and dried for about 1 hour.

Alternatively, dry the mint in the oven by warming the oven just barely for a minute at its lowest temperature, and then turn the oven off (any more heat than this, and the mint will turn too brown). Place the leaves in a single layer on a sheet pan and leave them in the oven to dry overnight, or for about 12 hours.

Store the mint in an airtight jar in the pantry for several months. It will lose its flavor over time, so it is most vibrant in the month after it is made.

Toasted Sesame Seeds

Sesame seeds gain delicious nutty flavor, color, and depth when they're toasted, so I like to toast lots of them right away when I buy big bags of them, then keep them on hand that way. Toasting sesame seeds takes some vigilance because the tiny seeds can burn easily, so it's best to toast at least a cup at a time.

Makes 1 cup / 300 g

1 cup / 200 g, or more, sesame seeds

Preheat the oven to 350°F / 175°C with a rack in the middle position and line a sheet pan with parchment paper. Spread the sesame seeds on the parchment and bake for about 6 minutes. Watch them closely to avoid burning them, stirring the seeds every 2 minutes until they are golden brown. Cool the seeds completely. To transfer the seeds to a jar or bowl, lift the long sides of the parchment from the pan and pour the seeds from the parchment into the container. Store the toasted sesame seeds in an airtight jar, either in the pantry or the refrigerator, for up to several months.

Butter Toasted Pine Nuts and Almonds

Nuts toasted in butter add so much richness and texture to any dish, especially Chicken Rice Pilaf with Butter Toasted Almonds (page 124), Spinach Pies (page 198), Open-Faced Lamb Pies (page 201), and to garnish grains, vegetables, and salads. I make at least a cup at a time and keep the nuts in an airtight container in the freezer, at the ready. Toasting the nuts in butter is a favorite way of the Lebanese, who often call them "fried nuts." In addition to flavor, butter toasting imparts even, golden color.

Makes 1 cup / 110 g

½ tablespoon salted butter

1 cup / 110 g slivered almonds or whole pine nuts

Fine sea salt, to taste

Melt the butter in a large skillet over medium heat. Add the nuts and reduce the heat to medium-low. Stir the nuts to coat them with the butter and continue stirring constantly until the nuts are golden brown. Keep a close watch over the nuts; they can burn quickly once they begin to brown.

Transfer the nuts to a bowl while they are still warm and salt them lightly. When they have cooled to room temperature, store the nuts in an airtight container in the refrigerator for a month or in the freezer for up to one year.

Tahini-Yogurt Sauce

This special sauce is excellent with Fresh Herb Falafel (page 142), grilled chicken, fish, or as a dip for crudité. Give it some heat with a chopped jalapeño pepper. Make the sauce vegan by replacing the yogurt with about ½ cup / 120 mL of cool water and increasing the tahini to ¾ cup / 180 mL.

Makes 1 generous cup / 240 mL

¾ cup / 170 g yogurt

⅓ cup / 80 mL tahini (well-stirred before measuring)

1 teaspoon kosher salt

1 small garlic clove, minced

Juice of 1 lemon

Process the yogurt, tahini, salt, and garlic in the food processor, or whisk in a medium mixing bowl, until combined. Add the lemon juice and pulse or whisk to combine. Taste and adjust the seasonings, if needed, so that the sauce has the nutty flavor of tahini with a bit of the tang of the yogurt.

Garlicky Mint Yogurt Sauce

This sauce is excellent as a dressing for greens, as well as with grilled meats, salmon, or as a dip for crudité. To make the sauce thicker to use as a dip, hold back on some of the lemon juice. Great additions include chopped jalapeño pepper, chopped scallions, or a couple of tablespoons of very finely chopped or grated cucumber.

Makes 1 generous cup / 240 mL

1 cup / 230 g labneh (page 29), or substitute Greek yogurt

Juice of ½ lemon

1 teaspoon crushed dried mint

1 tablespoon finely chopped fresh mint

1 teaspoon kosher salt

1 garlic clove, minced

In a small bowl, whisk the labneh and lemon juice until smooth. Stir in the dried and fresh mint, salt, and garlic. Chill the sauce for a couple of hours to allow the flavors to develop before serving if there's time, but it will still be delicious served immediately.

Lemon Vinaigrette

I like to call our Lemon Vinaigrette the little black dress of dressings—my go-to that always fits the bill. This is the perfect light dressing for virtually any salad, or to dress tomatoes garnished with mint or basil. The granulated garlic is a surprisingly delicious way to impart the flavor of garlic subtly to the dressing, the way my mother always makes it (page 80).

Makes about ⅓ cup / 80 mL

Juice of 1 to 2 lemons

2 teaspoons kosher salt

1 teaspoon granulated garlic powder

Freshly ground black pepper, to taste (about 5 grinds)

¼ cup / 60 mL extra-virgin olive oil

In a small bowl, combine the lemon juice, salt, garlic powder, and pepper. Slowly drizzle the olive oil into the lemon juice mixture, whisking constantly to emulsify the vinaigrette. Set the vinaigrette aside for at least 15 minutes to allow the flavors to develop. Whisk everything together again, taste, and add more lemon if needed.

Pita Chips

If you have thin, large Lebanese pita (page 243), those make wonderfully light, crisp chips that you can't stop eating. The chips are great fried or baked; both methods are here. Pita chips are delicious as a dipper with Whipped Hummus (page 49), Baba Gannouj (page 68), Labneh Dip with Crushed Red Pepper and Mint (page 51), or in salads like Fattoush Salad (page 84). They're also delicious sprinkled with za'atar or sumac, either right after frying or before baking when the bread is coated with oil.

Makes 8 servings

2 (10-inch / 25 cm) thin pitas or 3 (5-inch / 13 cm) thicker pitas

2 to 4 cups / 475 to 950 mL neutral oil, such as safflower or canola, if frying, or 3 tablespoons, if baking

Fine sea salt, to taste

Open the pitas and pull the halves apart along the seams, and then, using kitchen shears, cut the pita into 1-inch / 2.5 cm strips. Cut the strips into 2-inch / 5 cm pieces.

If you're frying the pita chips, heat the oil in a medium, tall-sided skillet or a 2-quart / 2 L saucepan over medium-high heat to 325°F / 160°C. The oil is ready when a tiny piece of pita bubbles vigorously and floats to the top of the oil.

Fry the pita in batches until they are light golden brown, about 15 seconds (they fry very quickly). Remove the chips with a slotted spoon to a paper towel-lined plate or sheet pan and sprinkle liberally with salt while they are hot.

Alternatively, you can bake the pita chips. Preheat the oven to 375°F / 190°C. Toss the pita pieces numerous times in a large bowl with 3 tablespoons of oil and 1 teaspoon sea salt, until they are fully coated. Spread them out on a sheet pan and bake them until they are light golden brown, stirring a few times and rotating the pan, about 10 minutes for the thin pita and up to 15 minutes for the thicker pita. Store the chips in an airtight container for a couple of weeks.

Za'atar Roasted Tomatoes

Roasting cherry tomatoes coaxes their sweetness out of them and takes the flavor and texture of even less-desirable winter tomatoes to entirely new heights. The addition of za'atar balances the tomatoes' sweetness and acidity with a wonderful earthiness and tang. Use them on crostini topped with labneh (page 29), on sandwiches, in salads (such as Crunchy Fennel Salad, page 85), or straight up on their own. Store the roasted tomatoes drizzled with olive oil in an airtight container in the refrigerator for about a week.

Makes 1 cup / 150 g

1 pint / 300 g cherry or grape tomatoes

2 tablespoons extra-virgin olive oil

½ teaspoon kosher salt

Freshly ground black pepper, to taste (about 5 grinds)

2 to 3 tablespoons za'atar, to taste

Line a heavy sheet pan with parchment paper. Slice the tomatoes in half. In a medium bowl, combine the tomatoes with the olive oil, salt, and pepper, and stir until they are well-coated. Place the tomatoes on the sheet pan cut-side up, and top each with a pinch of za'atar.

Arrange a rack in the center of the oven. Turn the oven on to 275°F / 135°C (no need to preheat when roasting like this), and roast the tomatoes for about 2 to 3 hours, depending on the size of the tomatoes. The tomatoes are done when they are meltingly soft and slightly shriveled. They can be used warm or cooled to room temperature.

Flower Water Syrup

These fragrant syrups are an essential part of many Lebanese pastries, and they're delicious in cold drinks and cocktails. For pastry like Walnut Baklawa Diamonds (page 158) and Knafeh with Melted Cheese and Orange Blossom Syrup (page 171), it is important to pour cold syrup over the hot pastry when it comes out of the oven, or to pour hot syrup over cooled pastry, or else the syrup won't absorb properly and the pastry will be soggy. I like to taste my pastry hot from the oven, so I always pour cool syrup over hot pastry so I can taste a piece from the pan right away without waiting for it to cool. Add the flower water a teaspoon at a time to gauge how much is needed; strength of flavor varies with different brands. You can double or halve the quantity of syrup easily, and store the syrup in an airtight container in the refrigerator for up to 3 months.

Makes 1 generous cup / 240 mL

1½ cups / 300 g granulated sugar

¾ cup / 180 mL water

Juice of ½ small lemon

2 teaspoons orange blossom water or ½ teaspoon rose water

In a small saucepan, combine the sugar with the water and the lemon juice and bring it to a boil over medium-high heat. Reduce the heat to low and simmer for 5 minutes. Remove the syrup from the heat and add the orange blossom water or rose water, tasting the syrup, and adding more a drop at a time if needed. Cool the syrup for about 30 minutes, and then pour it into a container, cover, and refrigerate it until it is completely cold, at least 1 hour.

Clarified Butter

There are a couple of good ways to clarify butter, and I use them both depending on how much time I have and what I'm using it for. Clarifying butter separates the milk solids from the pure butter fat, which is important when working with phyllo in particular because the solids burn, leaving dark spots. Clarified butter cooks at higher temperatures without burning. When I'm using melted clarified butter (as with the Phyllo Galette of Labneh, Caramelized Cherry Tomatoes, and Kalamata Olives, page 56, or the Walnut Baklawa Diamonds, page 158), I use the skim and strain method. When I need solid clarified butter (Shortbread Cookies, or *Graybeh*, page 164), I use the chill and rinse method, then bring the solid butter to room temperature. In either case, store any remaining clarified butter in an airtight container in the refrigerator for a couple of months or in the freezer for up to a year.

Makes 1⅓ cups / 360 g

1 pound / 450 g unsalted butter

The skim and strain method: Warm the butter in a small saucepan over low heat, undisturbed, until it is completely melted. Remove the pan from the heat and set it aside to rest, still undisturbed, for 30 minutes. Most of the solids will have fallen to the bottom of the pan. Use a spoon or small strainer to skim off and discard any solids that remain on the surface of the butter. Slowly pour the melted butter through a fine mesh sieve into a bowl, and stop pouring when you reach the solids at the bottom of the pan. There will be a teaspoon or so of melted butter surrounding the solids in the pan at this point; discard that with the solids. The strained clarified butter is ready to use.

The chill and rinse method: Melt the butter in a small saucepan over low heat, and then pour it, along with the solids, into a bowl. Chill the bowl in the refrigerator until it is firm, at least 3 hours. Once the butter is solid, run the bottom of the bowl under warm water to loosen the disk of butter, and then remove the disk and rinse the milky white solids off of the butter swiftly with warm water, patting the disk dry lightly with a clean cloth or paper towel.

Chickpeas

It may seem like overkill to peel chickpeas, but they are a must-have for all kinds of recipes where the skins simply don't belong. The skins cause grittiness and dampen flavor in hummus (page 49), and they fall off of chickpeas and are a nuisance in dishes like Freekeh with Tomato and Chickpeas (page 141) or Fava Beans and Chickpeas with Garlic, Lemon, and Olive Oil (page 145). Pre-peeled chickpeas are a game-changer because they eliminate the time and effort of peeling cooked chickpeas. Peeled chickpeas are available dried (page 242); they are par-cooked and don't need to be soaked like dry beans, but they do need to be cooked. Note that this recipe is specifically for par-cooked peeled chickpeas, and the timing won't work for their skin-on cousins.

Makes 2 cups / 300 g

1 cup / 200 g dry, peeled chickpeas

1 small yellow onion, peeled and quartered

1 teaspoon kosher salt

1 bay leaf

In a 3- or 4-quart / 3 or 4 L pot, cover the chickpeas by about 6 inches / 15 cm with water. Add the onion, salt, and bay leaf. Cover the pot and bring the water to a boil, staying close by so it doesn't boil over. Reduce the heat, remove the cover, and simmer on medium-low heat for about 90 minutes, or until the chickpeas are very tender to the bite, with a creamy quality. Add more water if it gets low at any point.

If you're making hummus, drain the chickpeas and discard the onion and bay leaf, reserving a cup of the cooking liquid. Use the chickpeas right away for any other dish, or refrigerate the chickpeas up to three days in their cooking liquid, so that they don't dry out, until you're ready to use them. At that point, drain the chickpeas, and reserve the cooking liquid if needed.

Peeled Chickpeas

To peel the skins from standard dried or canned chickpeas, baking soda helps get the job done.

For dry chickpeas, soak (overnight or quick-soak in boiling water for an hour), drain, and pat the chickpeas dry, and then stir in 1½ teaspoons of baking soda for every 2 cups / 400 g of chickpeas.

Warm the chickpeas in a 3- or 4-quart / 3 or 4 L pot over medium heat for 3 minutes, and then cover them with plenty of cool water and bring to a boil. Reduce the heat to medium-low and simmer for a few hours, or until the chickpeas are very soft. The skins will mostly fall off and can be poured away with the cooking water; remove any stragglers from the chickpeas with your fingers.

For canned chickpeas, drain and pat dry the chickpeas, and then stir in 1½ teaspoons of baking soda for every 2 cups / 400 g. Warm the coated chickpeas in the microwave or on the stove in a large skillet over medium heat for 3 minutes, and then rinse them with water in a large bowl three times. With each rinse, rub the chickpeas vigorously between your hands, and the skins will fall off and rinse away.

Maza & Salads

Whipped Hummus with
Minced Lamb and Sumac

Labneh Dip with
Crushed Red Pepper and Mint

Za'atar Roasted Tomato Crostini
with Labneh

Labneh Cheese Preserved in Olive Oil

Phyllo Galette of Labneh, Caramelized
Cherry Tomatoes, and Kalamata Olives

Poached White Asparagus
with Lemon and Pistachio Oil

Tahini Avocado

Warm Dates with Almonds
and Lime Zest

Garlicky Leeks with Cilantro in Olive Oil

Fried Cauliflower with Tahini Sauce

Mahogany Eggplant with
Labneh and Pomegranate

Za'atar Kale Chips

Baba Gannouj
(Smoky Eggplant Tahini Dip)

Pink Deviled Eggs with Yogurt and Mint

Muhammara
(Roasted Red Bell Pepper–Walnut Dip)

Spicy Cilantro Potatoes

Butter Lettuce with Walnut Vinaigrette

Warm Potato Salad with
Lemon and Mint

Avocado Tabbouleh in Little Gems

Yogurt–Cucumber Salad

Maryalice's Big Romaine Salad

Tomato and Sweet Onion Salad

Fattoush Salad

Crunchy Fennel Salad

Whipped Hummus with Minced Lamb and Sumac

It started years ago, my quest for ultra-smooth, light hummus. For a time I added a spoonful of yogurt to give my hummus a lift, and then I discovered that the culprit of my grainy hummus texture was the skin on the chickpeas. From then on, the skins had to go—but this can be a painstaking task. You can imagine my excitement, then, when my friend Sofia mentioned, casually!, that she makes her hummus with *pre-peeled* chickpeas. *You what?!* I made her repeat every word, along with where I could get them so that I could share them with hummus makers everywhere (page 242). I've been hugging her ever since. Now my homemade hummus is always all that I knew it could be: luscious, whipped, and perfectly smooth. Topped with chewy spiced lamb and herbs, this becomes *hummus kwarma* (HUM-moos KWAR-ma), a dish of succulent textural contrast and meaty flavor.

Makes 6 servings

For the hummus:

2 cups / 300 g cooked skinless chickpeas (see page 42), cooking liquid reserved

1 garlic clove, minced

½ cup / 120 mL tahini (well-stirred before measuring)

½ teaspoon kosher salt

Juice of 1 lemon

½ to 1 cup / 120 to 240 mL chickpea cooking liquid, as needed, or cold water

For the lamb:

1 pound / 450 g lamb shoulder meat

Juice of 1 lemon

2 garlic cloves, minced

1 teaspoon kosher salt

3 tablespoons sumac, divided

2 tablespoons extra-virgin olive oil, divided, plus more for finishing

1 tablespoon salted butter

¼ teaspoon ground cinnamon

¼ cup / 40 g pine nuts, toasted (page 33)

Few sprigs chopped fresh flat-leaf parsley

10 fresh mint leaves, cut in chiffonade

Thin pita or flatbread, for serving

Recipe Continues On Next Page

In the bowl of a food processor, puree the chickpeas and garlic until a thick paste forms (the paste will ball up a bit). With the machine running, slowly add the tahini, ½ teaspoon salt, and lemon juice. Then slowly add the cooled cup of cooking water or cold tap water (use this if your chickpeas are canned) until the hummus is very smooth and light, holding back on a little water and tasting the hummus as you go; you may not need all of it. Taste and add more salt and lemon if needed. Place the hummus in a bowl, cover, and refrigerate for up to a week. Bring the hummus back to room temperature for about 30 minutes before serving, reviving it with some lemon juice if needed.

For the minced lamb, chop the lamb shoulder into 1-inch / 2.5 cm pieces, cutting away excess fat and gristle. In a medium bowl, combine the lamb with the lemon juice, minced garlic, salt, 1 tablespoon of the sumac, and 1 tablespoon of the olive oil. Stir well and let the mixture marinate for 30 minutes at room temperature. Drain the meat and dry it off by patting lightly with a paper towel.

In a large skillet, heat 1 tablespoon of the oil and butter over medium-high heat until the butter melts and foams. Add the meat to the pan and sauté over high heat 5 to 10 minutes, or until the meat is completely browned and caramelized (the meat won't caramelize if it's crowded; brown it in batches if needed). Season the lamb with 1 tablespoon of the sumac and the cinnamon. Taste and adjust the seasonings.

Spoon the hummus onto six small (4- to 6-inch / 10 to 15 cm) plates, spreading the hummus with the back of the spoon to form a well in the center. Fill the well with a big spoonful of the lamb. Garnish the meat and hummus with the pine nuts, parsley, mint, the remaining sumac, and a drizzle of olive oil. Serve immediately with thin pita or flatbread.

Labneh Dip with Crushed Red Pepper and Mint

This is my all-time favorite way to eat labneh for breakfast. The heat-level of the crushed red pepper is completely up to you, but the combination of the hot pepper with the creamy labneh and mint . . . wow, time to wake up and taste the day. The labneh is delicious spread onto za'atar flatbread (page 190), for a classic Lebanese breakfast that includes olives, tomato wedges, and cucumber slices. Of course, labneh dip is great served anytime with vegetables, crostini, breads, or pita chips (page 37), or anything you can think of to dip in.

Makes 4 servings

2 cups / 460 g labneh (page 29), or substitute Greek yogurt

¼ teaspoon kosher salt

1 teaspoon crushed red pepper flakes

1 teaspoon crushed dried mint

A few fresh mint leaves, cut in chiffonade

Few sprigs fresh mint, for garnish

Extra-virgin olive oil, for drizzling

In a small mixing bowl, whisk the labneh, salt, and a teaspoon of cold water until it is smooth and creamy.

Using the back of a large metal spoon, spread the labneh on a 6- to 8-inch / 15 to 20 cm serving plate, making a swirl on top of the labneh with the back of the spoon. Sprinkle the red pepper flakes over the entire surface of the labneh. Crush the dried mint between your palms and dust the labneh with it, along with the chiffonade of fresh mint. Garnish with the tops of the mint sprigs in the center of the labneh, and finish with a drizzle of olive oil.

Za'atar Roasted Tomato Crostini with Labneh

The tomatoes take a couple of hours to roast, but they can be made ahead by several days and stored in an airtight container in the refrigerator; just don't eat them all up before making these! It's tempting, so I always roast a lot of tomatoes and keep them on hand for sandwiches, salads, pastas, and to eat just as they are. Assemble the crostini just before serving.

Makes 16 crostini

1 long, narrow baguette

¼ cup / 60 mL extra-virgin olive oil

2 tablespoons za'atar

1 teaspoon kosher salt

Few grinds of black pepper

1 cup / 230 g labneh (page 29), or substitute Greek yogurt

1 recipe Za'atar Roasted Tomatoes (page 38)

To make the crostini, heat the oven to 350°F / 175°C. Thinly slice the baguette into ½-inch / 1.5 cm slices. Brush both sides of the bread slices with olive oil, and season them lightly with za'atar, salt, and pepper. Arrange the slices on a sheet pan and bake for about 10 minutes, turning them over when the tops are light golden brown and continuing to bake until the reverse sides are also golden.

Place a dollop of well-stirred labneh on each crostini. Top the labneh with two or three roasted tomato halves, then dust everything with more of the za'atar. Serve them immediately.

Labneh Cheese Preserved in Olive Oil

This yogurt cheese is rich, dense, and special. In Lebanon, the cheese is called *shankleesh* (shank-LEESH), and is mixed with hot spices or other savory seasonings and dried in the sun. Our draining process here starts with thick labneh, but you can start with yogurt and just drain it longer by about 12 hours. Use any amount of labneh or yogurt, adjusting the size of the jar and amount of olive oil accordingly.

Makes about 2 dozen labneh balls

1 recipe labneh (page 29), or substitute Greek yogurt

½ teaspoon kosher salt

Best-quality extra-virgin olive oil, as needed

Za'atar, cayenne pepper, or crushed dried mint, to taste

Place a colander in the sink or set it in a bowl or deep pot, and line it with fine cheesecloth. Spoon the labneh into the cloth and drain it for 12 hours. Transfer the labneh to a small bowl and stir in the salt.

Line a sheet pan with one layer of ink-free paper towel. Form the extra-thick labneh into balls the size of walnuts, about 2 inches / 5 cm, and place those on the prepared sheet pan. They'll be a little sticky and imperfect at this stage. Top the balls with another layer of paper towel. Leave them to continue to dry out (refrigerated or not) for another day, changing out the paper towels whenever they get saturated with the whey, two or three times.

Reshape the now-dry labneh balls in the palms of your hands to make them even rounder, and pack them loosely into a clean jar. Pour excellent-quality extra-virgin olive oil over the labneh balls until they are completely covered. Close the lid of the jar tightly and keep the labneh balls refrigerated for many months, up to a year, with the flavor becoming deliciously more complex over time.

To serve the labneh balls, bring the jar to room temperature to liquefy the chilled olive oil they are preserved in. Spoon out the balls and eat them topped with some of the preserving olive oil and dusted liberally with za'atar, cayenne pepper, or crushed dried mint. A few of each with different toppings make a beautiful cheese plate with olives and crackers. They're also wonderful crumbled over salads (with the spices or without) or spread, simply, on toast.

Phyllo Galette of Labneh, Caramelized Cherry Tomatoes, and Kalamata Olives

I have so much fun working with phyllo dough for Lebanese pastry that it inspires me to use the dough in lots of other ways. This rustic tart comes out of the oven so golden and gorgeous: it's a showstopper. Phyllo dough typically comes in two sizes: 9 x 14-inch / 23 x 35 cm sheets or 14 x 18-inch / 35 x 45 cm sheets. For this recipe, use the smaller-sized sheets if you can find them. To use larger phyllo, simply trim the short side a few inches so that there isn't too much phyllo dough around the edges of the galette. Serve the galette as an appetizer or with a salad as a light meal.

Makes one 10-inch / 25 cm galette

¾ cup / 170 g labneh (page 29), or substitute Greek yogurt

1 large garlic clove, minced

¼ teaspoon kosher salt

1 tablespoon olive oil, plus more for drizzling

1 cup / 150 g cherry tomatoes, halved

8 sheets frozen phyllo dough, thawed

½ cup / 120 g clarified butter, melted (page 41)

5 pitted kalamata olives, thinly sliced

A few chives, chopped

Preheat the oven to 375°F / 190°C. Line a heavy sheet pan with parchment paper.

In a small bowl, whisk the labneh, garlic, and salt. Set aside.

In a large sauté pan, heat the olive oil over medium heat. Sear the tomatoes cut-side down for 3 to 5 minutes, or until the tomatoes are caramelized and golden brown. Using tongs, gently remove the tomatoes to a plate, and set them aside.

Cover the phyllo dough with plastic wrap and a lightly dampened clean kitchen towel to prevent it from drying out as you work (quickly!). Place one sheet of phyllo on the prepared sheet pan and use a pastry brush to dab it with a thin coat of butter. The butter need not coat every inch of the phyllo perfectly. Place another sheet of phyllo on top of the buttered sheet rotated a half-turn in the opposite direction, so that the edges hang over the long side of the first sheet. Brush with butter, and repeat with the remaining sheets of phyllo, alternating the direction of the phyllo as it is placed over the last sheet.

Spoon the labneh into the center of the phyllo and spread into a circle, 8 to 10 inches / 20 to 25 cm. Arrange the caramelized tomatoes, cut-side up, in concentric circles on top of the labneh. Scatter the sliced olives over the tomatoes.

Lift one edge of the phyllo layers and fold it over the filling to form the start of a 3-inch / 7.5 cm edge. Repeat the folding, working your way all the way around the circle and folding each section that is lifted over the last section. Brush the phyllo lip generously with the remaining butter.

Bake the tart until the phyllo is crisp and golden brown, 25 to 30 minutes. Drizzle the center of the tart with olive oil and sprinkle with the chopped chives. Cut the tart into wedges and serve it warm or at room temperature.

Poached White Asparagus with Lemon and Pistachio Oil

The flavor of pistachio oil is so pure, the essence of one of the greatest of all nuts in both taste and green, grassy color. White asparagus and lemon are a natural on their own, but with pistachio nuts and oil, they are as sublime as the spring elements that produced them. White asparagus takes much longer to cook than green; there is no pleasure in an al dente white asparagus spear (too fibrous and difficult to cut). A diced avocado added to your plate of asparagus with the pistachios is very good too.

Makes 4 servings

1 pound / 450 g white asparagus

Juice of 1 lemon

1 teaspoon kosher salt

2 tablespoons shelled roasted, salted pistachios

4 teaspoons pistachio oil

Fine sea salt, to finish

Trim the asparagus by snapping the ends off at their natural break. Peel them from just beneath the tip to the end with a vegetable peeler.

Cover the asparagus with water in a large sauté pan. Squeeze the lemon into the pan and add the teaspoon of salt. Cover the pan and bring the water to a boil, and then reduce the heat to medium-low and simmer for about 20 minutes, or until a spear can be easily cut with a knife and fork. Drain and set the asparagus aside to cool.

Remove the thin papery skin on each pistachio to reveal the bright green nut underneath by rubbing the skin off of each nut between your fingers and thumb. Coarsely chop the pistachios.

Divide the asparagus among four individual salad plates, or pile them, all facing the same direction, on a platter. Sprinkle the pistachios across the center of the asparagus crosswise, forming a line. Drizzle everything with pistachio oil, and finish with the sea salt.

Tahini Avocado

These wonderful avocados are a play on the traditional Lebanese maza dish of mashed avocado with tahini. I love to eat my perfectly ripe, silky smooth avocados with minimal handling—so instead of mashing them, I slice and drizzle them with the equally silky, smooth tahini. Tahini avocados taste delicious with sliced tomatoes, olives, and flatbread.

Makes 4 servings

1 lemon

2 ripe avocados, cut into ½-inch / 1.5 cm slices

1 tablespoon extra-virgin olive oil

2 tablespoons tahini (well-stirred before measuring)

1 small garlic clove, minced

¼ teaspoon kosher salt

Pinch of toasted sesame seeds (page 32)

Slice the lemon in half. Arrange the avocados on a serving plate and squeeze the juice of half of the lemon over them. Drizzle the avocados generously with olive oil.

In a small bowl, whisk the tahini, the juice of the other lemon half, minced garlic, and salt. Add about a teaspoon of cold water, whisking until the dressing is thin enough to run in a stream off the end of the spoon. Taste and add more salt, lemon juice, or water as needed.

Drizzle the tahini sauce over the avocado, and sprinkle with the toasted sesame seeds. Serve immediately.

Warm Dates with Almonds and Lime Zest

Dates are one of the sweetest, most natural confections you can put in your mouth, and a classic Middle Eastern sweet. They remind me of brown sugar, of caramel . . . nature's caramel. I learned about these almond-stuffed dates with lime at Tante Marie's Cooking School in San Francisco, from the great chef, author, and teacher Tori Ritchie. She learned them from Patricia Wells on a culinary trip to Morocco. I'd buy fresh, big, chewy California Medjool dates every week from a stall at the Ferry Farmer's Market near the little culinary school, and I had to force myself to save them, rather than eating them all on my hilly walk home, so I could eat them warm, stuffed with almonds, that evening. The dates are wonderful as an appetizer or after a meal (let your guests know there are almonds inside, not a pit!). The best dates to eat and to use for this recipe are fresh (not dried) Medjools, which happily are showing up regularly now in most grocery stores.

Makes 12 stuffed dates

12 Medjool dates

24 whole roasted, salted almonds, toasted

1 teaspoon extra-virgin olive oil

Sea salt, to finish

Grated zest of 1 organic lime

Pull open the tip of each date with your fingertips and pull out the pit. Push two almonds into the cavity and close the opening back together. The dates may look and feel messy at first, but they are malleable back to their original shape.

To warm the dates, heat the olive oil over medium-low heat in a skillet. Add the dates and cook, shaking the pan so they are lightly coated in oil and warmed through, about 2 minutes. Place the dates on a platter and sprinkle with salt and lime zest, and serve them right away, warm.

Garlicky Leeks with Cilantro in Olive Oil

I was surprised to find a version of these leeks in one of my old Lebanese cookbooks, since leeks aren't often used in traditional Lebanese cooking. But the way the dish allows the flavor of the leeks to shine, and makes such good use of olive oil, strikes me as very much Lebanese. Cilantro, I've discovered, is a beloved herb in lots of old-school Lebanese dishes. I've been more than happy to embrace this tradition, since I love anything with cilantro and I enjoy putting it to use Lebanese-style. If you don't, you are far from alone, and you can use parsley or mint instead.

Makes 6 servings

2 tablespoons kosher salt

3 large leeks

¼ cup / 60 mL extra-virgin olive oil

3 garlic cloves, minced

½ teaspoon ground coriander

¼ cup / 4 g finely chopped fresh cilantro, divided

Sea salt and freshly ground black pepper

Bring a medium saucepan of water to a boil and add the kosher salt.

Slice the leeks in half lengthwise to clean them, removing the outermost layer if it's dirty and rinsing them with plenty of cold running water to wash away all the grit and dirt. Rinse until the water runs clean. Slice the white and pale green parts of the leeks crosswise into 2-inch / 5 cm chunks (which will fall apart into separate pieces when poached).

In a small skillet, heat the olive oil over medium heat until it is hot, but not smoking. Turn down the heat, add the garlic and cook it for about 30 seconds, or just until fragrant. Add the coriander and all but about 1 tablespoon of the cilantro and cook for another 30 seconds. Remove the pan from the heat and season the garlic-cilantro oil lightly with a pinch of sea salt and a grind or two of black pepper.

Add the leeks to the boiling water and reduce the heat to medium-low. Simmer until the leeks are just tender to the bite with a hint of resistance, about 4 minutes; take care not to overcook the leeks, otherwise they will "melt" and fall apart. Taste a leek every minute or so to determine when they are done.

Drain the leeks thoroughly and add them to the olive oil mixture, stirring gently. Serve immediately, garnished with more cilantro and salt.

Fried Cauliflower with Tahini Sauce

Whenever my mother reminisces about her mother's cooking, it is the fried cauliflower that comes to mind first (secondly: pie, of every sort). My grandmother Alice Abowd fried batch after batch of crisp, light florets and piled the golden results on a big platter. Placed in the middle of her happy yellow Formica kitchen table, the fried cauliflower was the siren call for the family to come to the kitchen for dinner. The tahini sauce here is something special too, with the creamy tahini imparting a terrific contrast to the fried cauliflower. Be sure the cauliflower is bone-dry before frying it in the hot oil.

Makes 6 servings

1 head cauliflower

3 tablespoons plus 1 teaspoon kosher salt, divided

½ cup / 120 mL tahini (well-stirred before measuring)

1 small garlic clove, minced

¼ cup / 60 mL water, plus more as needed

Juice of 1 lemon

Few sprigs chopped fresh flat-leaf parsley leaves

Neutral oil for frying, such as safflower or canola

To prepare the cauliflower, remove the core by cutting around it at an angle with a chef's knife. Rinse the cauliflower, and then cut off florets 2 to 3 inches / 5 to 7.5 cm in size.

Fill a large pot with water to a few inches below the top, and bring the water to a boil. Add 3 tablespoons of salt, and blanch the cauliflower for about 3 minutes, just until the florets are al dente, stirring once or twice. Drain the cauliflower and spread the florets out on a clean kitchen towel or paper towel to dry, 30 to 45 minutes. Pat the cauliflower dry with another towel. The florets must be completely dry before frying (water can cause the hot oil to splatter).

For the tahini sauce, use a blender or a food processor for the lightest texture, or whisk it by hand. Combine the tahini, garlic, and 1 teaspoon salt in the blender or bowl. With the blade running, or as you whisk, slowly add the water and the lemon juice, stopping to scrape the sides of the bowl down, and tasting to adjust the seasonings.

Stir in the parsley. Cover and set the sauce aside or refrigerate it if you're waiting more than a couple of hours to serve it. A tablespoon of water or lemon juice may need to be added to thin it before serving.

In a medium pot, heat about 3 inches / 7.5 cm of oil to 375°F / 190°C, or until a small test sample of cauliflower or parsley bubbles immediately and vigorously in the oil. Add the florets to the hot oil with a slotted spoon in batches of 5 or 6 at a time. Fry the florets until they are light golden brown, turning them with a slotted spoon for even frying. Remove them from the oil with the slotted spoon and drain them on a paper towel-lined dish or sheet pan, sprinkling them with salt while they're hot. Return the oil to 375°F / 190°C again before adding more cauliflower. Be sure to maintain steady heat throughout the frying process, increasing and decreasing the heat as needed.

Serve the fried cauliflower hot, with the tahini sauce on the side.

Mahogany Eggplant with Labneh and Pomegranate

Purple is the color of royalty, and the Lebanese bow down to eggplant accordingly, making it the crowned prince of many succulent dishes. Though it always tastes wonderful, cooked eggplant often becomes something far less than royal in its looks. But thickly sliced eggplant brushed with a glossy pomegranate-olive oil coating and broiled brings out an alluring, mouthwatering shade of mahogany. Top that deep golden brown with snow-white labneh and ruby-red pomegranate seeds, and we're back on the throne again, both in looks and taste. Choose firm, heavy eggplant without a hint of give when squeezed.

Makes 4 servings

¼ cup / 60 mL extra-virgin olive oil

¼ cup / 60 mL pomegranate molasses

1 large (8 x 5-inch / 20 x 12 cm) eggplant

Fine sea salt

¾ cup / 170 g labneh (page 29), or substitute Greek yogurt

Handful of pomegranate seeds, for garnish

Line a rimmed sheet pan with parchment paper. Place an oven rack on the second shelf from the top, for broiling.

In a small bowl, whisk the olive oil and pomegranate molasses to fully blend and emulsify the mixture.

Cut off the stem and bottom of the eggplant, leaving the skin on. Cut the eggplant in half crosswise. Turn the eggplant halves flat-side down, and slice them lengthwise into 2-inch- / 5 cm thick wedges, about eight in total. For the end slices that are mostly skin, trim away most of the skin.

Place the eggplant slices on the prepared sheet pan, tucking them close together if needed. Coat both sides of the eggplant slices with the olive oil–pomegranate molasses mixture. Sprinkle both sides lightly with salt.

Broil the eggplant under a high broiler until the slices are deep mahogany brown, using a spatula to gently flip the now-fragile eggplant, about 8 minutes on the first side and 5 minutes on the other side (some moisture will be released as the eggplant cooks). Cool the eggplant to room temperature.

Whisk the labneh with a pinch of salt in a small bowl until it is smooth and creamy. Arrange the eggplant slices on a serving platter and top the center of each slice with a small dollop of labneh, about a tablespoon each. Sprinkle the eggplant and the labneh with the pomegranate seeds, and serve immediately.

HOW TO SEED A POMEGRANATE
(KINDLY, GENTLY)

My pomegranate love reaches far back to when I was a small child: I am sitting on the kitchen counter, at home on Wagon Wheel Lane, snugly next to the sink. Uncle Joe, is visiting from California: Joe Abood, my *Jiddo's* (my grandfather's) brother. We loved Uncle Joe, and though I could not have been more than 6 years old, I remember the lines of his face, and his raspy voice. Perhaps he lifted me up onto the counter so that I could watch him at work with the beautiful fruit he'd brought from California. Perhaps my mother said, *Keep her close to the sink so we don't get pomegranate juice all over the kitchen.* Yes, probably.

Uncle Joe's hands were the sort a child trusts, old knobby hands that contain knowledge, memory, and other secrets. Deep in the white porcelain sink, he pulled apart the radiant pomegranate, which then, 40 years ago, was a real wonder, a mystery, not a fruit we could pick up at the market whenever we wanted. Uncle Joe had pulled the garnet globes from the trees in his own California yard, wrapped them in his nightshirt and slacks, and put them in his suitcase to bring to Michigan, a gift. Because the Lebanese, we most of the time have fruit on our minds.

He worked the well-traveled pomegranate to remove the white membrane and reveal the gems underneath. *Eat*, he said. Did Uncle Joe speak English? I don't think so. I don't recall much talking, just a language of hands and fruit and flavor. I followed his lead when he didn't spit out the crunchy seeds, understanding that those were as good for the taking as the precious-little tart juice that surrounded them.

So now, when I see the pomegranates being handled with such harshness, cut in half and whacked with a wooden spoon until the fragile little seeds fall, stunned and many broken, into a bowl? I can't take it. Pomegranates deserve better.

Like so:

Core the flower end of the pomegranate at an angle all the way around it, and pull out the plug.

Cut the other end, the stem end, flat across the bottom.

Score the pomegranate along the subtle ridges of each lobe.

Gently pull apart the pomegranate, pulling one lobe away from the fruit. Peel away the white membrane to reveal the plump red seeds beneath. Use your fingers to gently loosen the seeds.

Use this same kind method with the rest of the grateful pomegranate.

Coddle your well-earned seeds in the refrigerator in a paper towel-lined container, with another paper towel on top of them, where they will repay you by staying nice for a couple of weeks.

Za'atar Kale Chips

Za'atar, at long last, is becoming a common spice mix in kitchens well beyond Lebanese ones. With good reason—the combination of earthy wild thyme, tangy sumac, and nutty sesame gives an irresistible zing to everything it seasons. I made kale chips for years before a light bulb went on and I started dusting them with a handful of za'atar. And now? Let's just say there's no going back to plain kale chips again. They are an ideal—and deliciously addictive—conduit for the za'atar, an addiction none of us has to curb. Taste your za'atar and if it's salty, no added salt is needed; if not, a pinch of salt over the kale will bring up the flavor nicely.

Makes about 8 servings

1 bunch kale (any variety), washed and patted dry

2 tablespoons extra-virgin olive oil

3 tablespoons za'atar

Kosher salt, if needed

Line two sheet pans with parchment paper or foil. Place the racks in the top and lower third of the oven, and preheat the oven to 300°F / 150°C.

Trim the kale by stripping the leaf away from the tough stem that runs in a vein up the center. Tear the kale into 3- or 4-inch / 7.5 to 10 cm pieces. Place the kale on the sheet pans and drizzle each sheet with a tablespoon of the olive oil. Mix the kale and oil with your hands until all of the kale is thoroughly coated. Spread the kale out in a single layer on the sheet pans, and dust it liberally with za'atar, as well as the kosher salt, if needed.

Bake for 20 minutes, rotating the sheet pans top to bottom and front to back halfway through. The chips will darken and shrivel; also taste a chip to see if it has crisped up, baking another minute or two if not. Cool the chips to room temperature, and store them in an airtight container for up to a week.

Maza & Salads

Baba Gannouj (Smoky Eggplant Tahini Dip)

Baba means "father" in Arabic (and I loved calling my dad that)—so just for the reference to Dad alone do I love baba gannouj, notwithstanding the wonderful smoky flavor of char-roasted eggplant. In the Middle East this dip is often called *moutabbal*, and while their baba gannouj includes walnuts and pomegranate molasses, I'm sticking with what so many of us know and love as baba gannouj. Select eggplant that is very firm when squeezed, and fairly narrow, which often means fewer seeds. The bitter baba you may have tasted now and then is attributable to the cook not removing the seeds from the eggplant before mashing it up. Do that, and you'll have a much different, far superior baba gannouj. Use at least two eggplants since removing the seeds reduces the amount of eggplant you have left to work with. The pomegranate seeds add vibrant color to the—shall we say, otherwise homely?—dip, and a delicious tart flavor too. Serve with pita bread, pita chips, or vegetables.

2 (8 x 5-inch / 20 x 12 cm) firm eggplants

3 to 4 tablespoons tahini (well-stirred before measuring), or as needed

1 teaspoon / 6 g kosher salt

1 garlic clove, minced

Juice of ½ lemon

Few grinds of black pepper

Extra-virgin olive oil, for drizzling

Handful of pomegranate seeds (page 66)

Preheat a grill, a gas burner, or the broiler on high. Poke a few holes in the eggplants with a knife or skewer (so the skin won't burst). Char the eggplants on all sides, 15 to 20 minutes. If you're broiling the eggplants, place them on a parchment-lined baking sheet a few inches from the heat source. Turn them over halfway through cooking (using tongs) to char them evenly. When the skin is blistered and the eggplants are very soft, remove them from the heat.

When they are cool enough to handle, peel the skin off with your fingers and cut away the stem end. Open the eggplant and pull out the lines of seeds and discard them.

Chop or mash the remaining eggplant in a medium bowl. Add the tahini, salt, garlic, lemon juice, and black pepper. Taste and adjust the seasonings if needed, and then spoon the baba gannouj onto a plate. Make some swirls in the eggplant with the back of the spoon, and drizzle olive oil over the top. Sprinkle with pomegranate seeds and serve.

Pink Deviled Eggs with Yogurt and Mint

These pink deviled eggs are beautiful, and whenever I'm presented with such beauty, I am torn between eating them and just looking at them. Beets give the eggs their light pink shade in a quick pickling process, and yogurt flavors the egg yolk with more delicious zing than mayonnaise alone. The pink, yellow, and green mint hues brighten any table these eggs grace.

Makes 16 deviled eggs

8 large eggs

1 teaspoon baking soda

½ beet, trimmed, peeled, and cut into 1-inch / 2.5 cm wedges

1 cup / 240 mL white vinegar

2 whole cloves

3 tablespoons laban (page 26) or plain yogurt

1 tablespoon mayonnaise

½ teaspoon yellow mustard

¼ teaspoon kosher salt

A few fresh mint leaves, cut in chiffonade

In a large saucepan, cover the eggs with cool water by 1 inch / 2.5 cm, and add the baking soda. Bring to a boil, and then remove the pan from the heat. Cover the pan with a tight-fitting lid and let the eggs sit, off the heat, for 16 minutes.

Run cool water over the eggs until they cool substantially. Crack the eggs on both ends, and then gently roll them on the counter under the palm of your hand to crush the shell. Peel the eggs under cool running water, starting at the large end of the egg to get under the membrane.

To lightly pickle the eggs, place the eggs tightly in a small bowl or jar with beet wedges. Combine the vinegar, cloves, and ½ cup / 120 mL water in a small saucepan. Bring just to a boil, and then pour the hot brine over the eggs and beet to completely submerge the eggs. Pickle the eggs for about 2 hours at room temperature for a light pink color that only penetrates slightly into the egg white's edge.

To stuff the eggs, slice them in half lengthwise and remove the yolks. In a small bowl, mash the yolks thoroughly with a fork, breaking up as many lumps as possible. Stir in the yogurt, mayonnaise, and mustard thoroughly. Taste and season with salt, adding more yogurt if needed to make the filling loose enough to dollop but still thick enough to hold its shape.

Fill each of the egg halves with the yolk mixture. Sprinkle the mint over the eggs and serve, or cover and chill until serving.

Muhammara
(Roasted Red Bell Pepper–Walnut Dip)

The more you make this wonderful dip, the more you will adjust the spices to your own liking. A jar of roasted red bell peppers will work just as well as roasting your own. This is delicious as a dip with fresh pita (page 192) or pita chips (page 37), or as a sauce, spooned atop chicken, grilled meats, or fish. Muhammara will keep, refrigerated in an airtight container, for about a week.

Makes about 3 1/3 cups / 575 g

2 red bell peppers, trimmed, roasted, and peeled

1 cup / 120 g walnut pieces, toasted

2/3 cup / 40 g fresh breadcrumbs or panko, toasted

2 teaspoons pomegranate molasses

2 garlic cloves

Pinch of red pepper flakes

Juice of 1/2 lemon

1 teaspoon paprika

1/2 teaspoon ground cumin (optional)

1 teaspoon kosher salt

Few grinds of black pepper

1/4 cup / 60 mL extra-virgin olive oil, plus more for serving

Combine the peppers and walnuts in a food processor and pulse until the mixture is smooth. Add the breadcrumbs, pomegranate molasses, garlic, red pepper flakes, lemon juice, paprika, cumin (if using), salt, and pepper, processing to combine. With the processor running, add the olive oil slowly and blend until the oil is completely incorporated. Turn off the processor and scrape down the sides of the processor bowl as you go.

Serve the muhammara drizzled with olive oil in a small bowl, chilled or at room temperature.

Spicy Cilantro Potatoes

So many cultures make and love their spicy potato dishes, and the Lebanese are no different. *Batata harra* (bah-TAH-tuh HAR-ruh) is a classic Lebanese plate of fried potatoes tossed in spicy, garlicky herbed olive oil. They're perfect on their own, or served with a simple cool sauce of labneh mixed with lemon.

Makes 8 servings

Neutral oil for frying, such as safflower or canola

4 medium russet potatoes, peeled and cut into 1-inch / 2.5 cm chunks (4 cups)

2 tablespoons extra-virgin olive oil

1 teaspoon kosher salt

1 large garlic clove, minced

Few sprigs chopped fresh cilantro leaves

½ teaspoon red pepper flakes

In a medium-size deep, heavy saucepan, pour the oil to a depth of about 3 inches / 7.5 cm and place over medium heat. Bring the temperature to 375°F / 190°C. Line a plate or sheet pan with paper towel.

The oil is ready when a bit of cilantro dropped in bubbles vigorously and floats to the top. Fry the potatoes in batches until they are golden brown, transferring them with a slotted spoon to the prepared plate. Bring the oil back to temperature before frying each batch, keeping the heat steady by adjusting the temperature as needed.

In a medium serving bowl, combine the olive oil, salt, garlic, all but a pinch of the cilantro, and red pepper flakes. Add the hot potatoes and toss to coat them completely with the herbed oil. Sprinkle with the remaining cilantro and serve immediately.

Butter Lettuce with Walnut Vinaigrette

When I finished my graduate degree in literature, I was invited back to my undergraduate alma mater, Saint Mary's College at Notre Dame, to teach for a semester. I was excited but a little nervous at 24 years old to be among my former professors, now as their colleague. One of my favorite teachers there invited me on day one to have dinner at his home, which gave me such a great feeling of warm welcome. I was fascinated to see my professor's interesting home, and everything I ate that night was vegetarian and extraordinary. My request for all of the recipes was met with an envelope full of them the next day. That included this quietly special salad that speaks to my Lebanese love of all things walnut.

Makes 6 servings

½ teaspoon kosher salt

1 tablespoon sherry vinegar

3 tablespoons walnut oil

1 small shallot, finely chopped

Few grinds of black pepper

1 head butter lettuce, washed and trimmed

2 tablespoons chopped walnuts, toasted

In a small bowl, dissolve the salt in the sherry vinegar. Whisk in the walnut oil until the mixture is emulsified. Stir in the chopped shallot and black pepper, and allow the vinaigrette to rest to deepen its flavors for at least 15 minutes.

Tear the lettuce into 2-inch / 5 cm pieces and place them in a serving bowl or on a serving platter. In a small bowl, mix the nuts with a teaspoon of the vinaigrette to give them a little gloss. Dress the lettuce lightly with the vinaigrette. Sprinkle the toasted walnuts over the lettuce and serve immediately.

Warm Potato Salad with Lemon and Mint

Here, my friends, is a shining example of all that is healthful about Lebanese cuisine: a potato salad that is low in fat but high in flavor, thanks to the combination of scallions, lemon, and mint. Think summer picnic, but also warm right from the stovetop as a delicious side dish for meats, fish, or sandwiches. Dress the potatoes while they're still very warm, but wait to add the mint until the potatoes have cooled a little—otherwise the mint will turn dark from the heat and will lose the beautiful green that makes the salad so pretty. This potato salad is as delicious the day after it is made; cover and refrigerate overnight, and then bring to room temperature and add more fresh mint, stirring gently.

Makes 8 servings

- 3 pounds / 1.5 kg russet potatoes, peeled and cut into ½-inch / 1.5 cm dice
- 2 teaspoons kosher salt, divided
- Juice of 3 lemons
- ¼ cup / 60 mL extra-virgin olive oil
- 1 bunch scallions, white and green parts, finely sliced
- 10 fresh mint leaves, cut in chiffonade

Place the potatoes in a large pot and cover by 1 inch / 2.5 cm with cold water. Add 1 teaspoon of salt. Cover and bring to a boil, and then remove the lid and reduce the heat to medium. After about 6 minutes, test a sample of the potatoes every minute or so with the tip of a paring knife. They are ready when the knife cuts into the potato with resistance, very al dente, about 12 minutes. Be careful not to overcook the potatoes or they will turn to mush when you stir them with the dressing.

Drain the potatoes and gently transfer them into a serving bowl. Season the warm potatoes with the remaining teaspoon of salt, lemon juice, and olive oil, stirring gently with a metal spoon. Taste and adjust the seasonings. When the potatoes have cooled down for 10 minutes, add the scallions and all but a tablespoon of the mint, stirring gently to combine. Top with more mint as a garnish.

Avocado Tabbouleh in Little Gems

There is perhaps no more identifiable Lebanese dish than our tabbouleh. It is a beloved salad with good reason: tabbouleh is an effort, and things that take an effort often have a high value and pay-off. The chopping load is big. If you're my sister, who considers any opportunity to chop a really fun time, that effort is a pleasure, and a gift to your eaters. If you're someone else (me), you really wish your sister were around all of the time to take care of the chop job. Tabbouleh was always a special-occasion salad at our house as a labor of love, and we always appreciated it for that (it is tempting to use the food processor to chop the parsley, but that method turns the parsley to mush quickly). Tabbouleh is all about its fresh parsley and mint flavor, with a supporting cast of tomatoes, onion, and a very little bit of bulgur (too often, misunderstood tabboulehs are more bulgur than herb). Traditionally tabbouleh is eaten with long leaves of romaine. I like to nestle my tabbouleh in tender Little Gem cups and to stud the salad with avocado, which loves all of the lemon in the dressing. Pick up the Little Gem boats filled with tabbouleh with your hands and eat them that way, casual and fun. You can prep the ingredients a day or two in advance and combine everything when you're ready to serve, making tabbouleh a much swifter affair.

Makes 8 servings

⅓ cup / 65 g bulgur, #1 fine grade

3 bunches curly parsley

1 pint cherry tomatoes, diced into ¼-inch / .5 cm pieces

1 ripe avocado, diced into ¼-inch / .5 cm pieces

5 scallions, sliced thinly crosswise

4 sprigs fresh mint leaves, finely chopped

Juice of 2 lemons

¼ cup / 60 mL extra-virgin olive oil

½ teaspoon kosher salt

¼ teaspoon granulated garlic powder

Freshly ground black pepper, to taste

2 heads Little Gem romaine, rinsed and dried

Recipe Continues On Next Page

Rinse the bulgur twice in a small bowl, letting the bulgur settle for a few seconds before pouring off the water. Add enough fresh water just to cover the bulgur. Soak it for 30 minutes, or until it is softened. Pour off and squeeze out any excess water.

While the bulgur softens, prepare the parsley. Wash the parsley by dunking and shaking it in a sink full of cool water two or three times, changing the water between rinses. Wrap the parsley in clean kitchen towels and gently squeeze, soaking up as much water as possible, and then change out the towels for dry ones and squeeze again. Or, dry the parsley in a salad spinner, and then squeeze it in towels to soak up any remaining water. The drier the parsley, the easier it will be to chop and the nicer the tabbouleh will be. If you are prepping the parsley in advance, which is ideal for dryness, let it sit out on the towels for a few hours after it has been patted dry, and then bundle the parsley up in paper towels and refrigerate it until you are ready.

Pinch off the curls of parsley from their stems. Chop the curls in two or three batches with a large chef's knife, gathering the parsley up as you chop to form a more compact mound, until it is finely chopped.

In a medium bowl, combine the parsley, tomato, avocado, scallions, mint, and bulgur. Stir in the lemon juice, olive oil, salt, garlic powder, and pepper. Taste and adjust the seasonings, adding more lemon and salt if needed. Let the tabbouleh rest for about 15 minutes so the bulgur will soak up, and be flavored by, the juices.

Pull the Little Gem leaves from their stems and arrange the nicest, cup-like leaves on a platter. Fill each cup with a big spoonful of the tabbouleh, and serve immediately.

Yogurt–Cucumber Salad

Summer . . . backyard garden . . . freshly mown grass . . . sunshine and blue sky. The fresh flavor of cucumber and yogurt always takes me to this place, no matter when I make this salad (which I do, all year long). This classic *laban khiyar* (luh-BIN kee-YAR) is fairly thin, so it's nice to serve it in small bowls. The flavors here develop over time, so make the salad a few hours or even a day ahead and chill it, if you can. This is delicious on its own or as a side dish with lamb, chicken, fish (especially salmon), lentils, grilled vegetables, or a hamburger: laban khiyar is so good that it might even take your mind off of French fries! The salad stays nice, and the cucumbers crunchy, for a good 4 days in the refrigerator.

Makes 6 servings

2 cups / 570 g plain, unsweetened whole milk yogurt (page 26)

1 garlic clove, minced

½ teaspoon kosher salt

Juice of ½ lemon

2 teaspoons crushed dried mint, plus more for garnish

5 fresh mint leaves, finely chopped

3 (4-inch / 10 cm) Kirby or Persian cucumbers

In a medium bowl, combine the yogurt with the garlic, salt, lemon juice, and dried and fresh mint.

Slice the cucumbers lengthwise into quarters to make four spears. Slice the spears crosswise into ¼-inch / .5 cm pieces. Add the cucumbers to the yogurt mixture. Taste and add more of anything the salad might need (I tend to want more dried mint). Let the salad rest for at least an hour and up to a week in the refrigerator. To serve, dust the top of the salad with crushed dried mint.

Maza & Salads

Maryalice's Big Romaine Salad

This salad has been on the family dinner table my whole life (did I eat it as a baby? I must have), just as it was on the table every night of my mother's life growing up in her family. No matter how much salad my mother makes, we eat it all. Her grandchildren, especially Maria, look forward to her salad whenever they come for dinner, and everyone hopes to be the one to finish the last scoop in the bowl at the end of dinner. My brother Dick, who is a great cook, discovered that leaving the onion out diminishes the overall flavor of the salad; better to leave them in for the flavor they impart, and let any onion-haters push them aside. Mom always squeezes the lemon directly over the salad, and while she tries, God love her, she never catches all of the seeds. I'm pretty sure my plate has been the recipient of every missed lemon seed, ever.

Makes 10 servings

2 heads romaine, washed, trimmed, and torn into big bite-sized pieces

2 large tomatoes, cut into 1-inch / 2.5 cm chunks

1 English cucumber, quartered lengthwise and thinly sliced

1 medium-size sweet onion, thinly sliced

Juice of 2 lemons

¼ cup / 60 mL extra-virgin olive oil

2 teaspoons kosher salt

2 teaspoons granulated garlic powder

Several grinds of black pepper

In a large salad bowl, combine the lettuce, tomatoes, cucumber, and onion. To dress the salad as my mother does, simply add each ingredient into the full salad bowl rather than mixing the vinaigrette separately. Squeeze the lemon juice over the top through your fingers, (ideally) catching the seeds to discard them. Drizzle the oil over the salad, and season with salt, garlic powder, and pepper. Toss the salad, taste it, and adjust the seasonings as needed. Serve immediately.

SALAD EVERY NIGHT

Eating in a restaurant just wasn't part of the program. In the mint green house on Maple Street where my mother grew up in Fostoria, Ohio, in the 1940s and '50s, dinner was at home. Always. When I press her on this every few years or so, she thinks long and hard, squinting her eyes as though blocking out everything in front of them might bring up a memory she may have left behind somewhere along the way.

It wasn't because they couldn't eat out, that she's made clear. It's that my grandparents had seven children to educate as far as they might like. Plus, my grandfather Richard worked late into the night at his New Ohio Hotel, and he split up the evening's long hours by coming home for a brief, yet full-on, dinner. This meant that my grandmother Alice cooked without respite. There wasn't a day when she would or could have sat back on the couch and said, *Let's go out tonight*. The image I have of Alice is one of constant motion. Hands, tiny hands befitting of her 4-foot-10-inch frame, in the mix all day, every day. A mind all about it too: what to cook, what to do with the leftovers, and how to cook, always, with economy and taste.

The anticipation of his dinner, I suppose, got my grandfather through the day and into the night behind the desk at the hotel. His wife's legendary cooking, and the welcome he'd receive from the two youngest (by far) of his children—this was his daily bread, as much as any of the flatbreads or talami whose aroma wafted up the street as he marched home for dinner.

In my grandmother's rotation of every Arabic and American dish you could want to eat, there were two things about the evening meal on Maple Street that were steadfast: a salad of romaine with lemon and olive oil, just as sure as where that meal would be eaten, at home (*I've had this salad every night of my life*, my mother likes to say). Secondly: the rosary, recited by everyone at the table the moment the last plate was cleared. The prayers weren't questioned. It's simply what they did, and that was that. Just like eating at home, the salad, its own kind of prayer bead that didn't wear from use, but more beloved for its reliability, its familiarity, its certain place at the table.

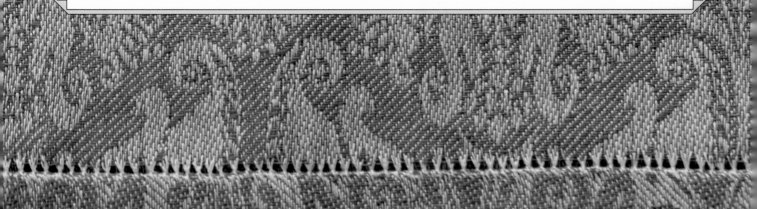

Tomato and Sweet Onion Salad

This is less of a recipe than it is a sketch of what belongs in a Lebanese tomato salad, which is so integral, so delicious that life just wouldn't be as good without it! If it is not tomato season and you want this salad, use halved Campari tomatoes or small grape or cherry tomatoes to avoid mealy winter tomatoes. You'll notice that it takes a hefty amount of mint to get its flavor to shine through. Tomato salad is especially good eaten with thin flatbread or thin pita bread: just pick up the salad with a small piece of bread and eat it that way. You may want a spoon to help you get all of the incredibly good juices into your mouth when the tomatoes are gone. . . .

Makes 6 servings

2 pounds / 900 g ripe tomatoes of any shape, size, or color (a variety is nice)

20 fresh mint leaves

1 medium-size sweet onion, very thinly sliced

Juice of 1 lemon

2 tablespoons extra-virgin olive oil

½ teaspoon granulated garlic powder

1 teaspoon kosher salt

Few grinds of black pepper

To slice the tomatoes, use a serrated knife and cut them in half through the core end. Cut out the cores. Slice the tomatoes into somewhat irregular 1-inch chunks rather than perfect wedges.

The mint can be torn into small pieces, or cut in chiffonade into thin ribbons.

Place the tomatoes, onion, and mint in a bowl. Add the lemon juice, olive oil, garlic powder, salt, and pepper. Combine and taste. Has your life been changed yet with how good this is? If not, let the salad rest for a bit, taste again, and adjust the seasonings to get you there.

Fattoush Salad

Like so many fattoush lovers the world over, I can eat this Lebanese bread salad every night of the week and still come back for more. This classic is a favorite for its crunchy pita chips, tart sumac, and crisp vegetables with romaine dressed in a perfect balance of tanginess and sweetness, owing to a vinaigrette of pomegranate molasses and lemon juice.

Makes 8 servings

Juice of 1 lemon

1 teaspoon pomegranate molasses

1 small garlic clove, minced

1 teaspoon kosher salt

2 teaspoons crushed dried mint, divided

2 teaspoons sumac, divided

3 tablespoons extra-virgin olive oil

2 hearts of romaine, chopped into 1- to 2-inch / 2.5 to 5 cm pieces

1 cup / 150 g cherry tomatoes, quartered

½ red onion, thinly sliced

2 radishes, thinly sliced

Pita chips (page 37)

10 fresh mint leaves, cut in chiffonade

Freshly ground black pepper

For the vinaigrette, in a small bowl whisk the lemon, pomegranate molasses, garlic, salt, 1 teaspoon of the dried mint, 1 teaspoon of the sumac, and olive oil until it is thoroughly combined and emulsified.

In a salad bowl, combine the romaine, tomatoes, onion, radishes, and pita chips. Dress the salad with the vinaigrette, tossing it to evenly coat everything. Dust the fattoush with the remaining sumac, dried mint, the fresh mint, and a few grinds of black pepper, and serve immediately.

Crunchy Fennel Salad

Licorice, black and red, was one of the basic food groups of my diet when I worked in the summers at the Abood Law Firm as a kid. My cousins and I made daily stops at The Peanut Shop when we were out running the office errands, the most important of these being my dad's request for a little bag of gumdrops. For me, though, it was always licorice, which came in the shop's own bags and was chewy and fresh. And while I'm still a fan, my food groups have changed a good bit (thankfully) and I love to get my anise fix from a gently flavored bulb of fennel, shaved thin and dressed in lemony labneh.

Makes 4 servings

1 fennel bulb with fronds, cleaned and patted dry

2 tablespoons labneh (page 29) or substitute Greek Yogurt

Juice of ½ lemon

1 tablespoon crushed dried mint

¼ teaspoon granulated garlic powder

¼ teaspoon kosher salt

Few grinds of black pepper

A few fresh mint leaves, torn or cut in chiffonade

2 tablespoons pine nuts, toasted

½ recipe Za'atar Roasted Tomatoes (page 38)

Extra-virgin olive oil, for drizzling

Trim the fennel by cutting across the top of the bulb to remove the fronds and stalks, and slicing away a thin layer along the bottom. Pinch off the wispy fronds and lightly chop them; set them aside for garnish. Cut the bulb in half from top to bottom, and cut out the small core on each half. Shave the fennel very thinly, as thinly as possible (⅛-inch / 3 mm wide at most), with a sharp knife or a mandoline set at 1.5 mm.

In a small bowl, whisk the labneh with the lemon juice and about a teaspoon of cold water to loosen the mixture. Add the dried mint, garlic powder, salt, and pepper.

Dress the fennel with the labneh mixture in a serving bowl, stirring until the fennel is evenly coated. Garnish the fennel with fresh mint, toasted pine nuts, and fennel fronds. Gently stir in the Za'atar Roasted Tomatoes, and drizzle the salad with olive oil to serve.

Main Dishes

Stuffed Vegetables

Cabbage Rolls in Garlic or Tomato Broth

Grape Leaves with Lemon

Stuffed Koosa in Tomato Broth

Stuffed Koosa with Yogurt and Mint

Eggplant with Lamb,
Tomato, and Pine Nuts

Kibbeh

Raw Kibbeh (Kibbeh Nayeh)
with Househ

Baked Kibbeh Sahnieh

Fried Kibbeh with Mint Butter

Vegan Tomato Kibbeh

Potato and Spinach Kibbeh
with Yogurt-Mint Sauce

Yogurt-Poached Kibbeh
with Parsley-Garlic Oil

Lamb, Chicken, Eggs, and Fish

Spiced Lamb Kofta Burgers

Roasted Leg of Lamb with
Black Cherry-Pomegranate Salsa

Green Bean and Lamb Stew

Grilled Lamb Skewers
with Fresh Mint Sauce

Fragrant Chicken Soup with Vermicelli

Yogurt Marinated Chicken Skewers
with Toum Garlic Sauce

Hushweh (Chicken Rice Pilaf with
Butter Toasted Almonds)

Zucchini, Parsley, and
Mint Omelets (Ijjeh)

Baked Eggs with Spinach,
Labneh, and Sumac

Olive Oil Fried Eggs with Za'atar

Pan-Seared Snapper with Tahini Sauce
and Toasted Pine Nuts

Pistachio-Crusted Whitefish
with Parsley-Lemon Butter

Cabbage Rolls in Garlic or Tomato Broth

I love to cook cabbage rolls stuffed with meat in delicate garlic broth, and I find cabbage rolls stuffed with bulgur or rice without meat are most flavorful if they're cooked in tomato broth. These rolls are especially good the second day, a great make-ahead dish.

Makes about 18 rolls

3 teaspoons kosher salt, divided

1 head green cabbage, cored

6 chicken wings or 3 bone-in pork chops (optional)

1 recipe Lamb, Bulgur, or Rice Stuffing (page 89)

1 large head garlic, cloves separated and peeled

¼ cup / 65 g tomato paste (if using Bulgur or Rice Stuffing)

Labneh (page 29), for serving

Bring an 8-quart / 7.5 L pot of water to a boil with 1 teaspoon of the salt, and blanch the whole head of cabbage in the boiling water for about 3 minutes. Remove the leaves one by one from the head with tongs, which will be easy to loosen as they soften and turn bright green and translucent. Leave the thicker, inner leaves an extra minute or two in the water to soften after pulling them from the head with the tongs. Place the cabbage leaves on a plate or sheet pan to cool as you remove them from the pot. For the thicker leaves, shave away a thin layer of the protruding rib with a sharp knife, so that those leaves will roll up more easily.

Line the bottom of the 8-quart / 7.5 L pot with the chicken wings, if using, and then top the chicken with a few cabbage leaves (use torn or small ones). Or, simply line the bottom of the pan with a couple of the torn or small cabbage leaves.

To stuff the leaves, place a leaf with the stem end nearest you and the interior or "cup" shape of the leaf facing up. Place about a tablespoon of the stuffing on a cabbage leaf at the stem end and spread the stuffing out lengthwise along the bottom of the leaf, like a finger. Roll up the leaf around the meat (no need to tuck in the edges). Stuff all of the leaves this way, placing each roll seam-side down in the prepared pan snugly against one another and tucking in the garlic cloves throughout as you go. Alternate the direction of the rows with each layer of stuffed leaves in the pot. Make small meatballs with any leftover meat stuffing (if using) and place those on top. Place a salad plate face-down over the rolls (and meatballs) to hold the rolls down while they cook. Fill the pot up to the plate with cold water and add 2 teaspoons of kosher salt to the water.

To make tomato broth (if using, for vegetable stuffings), whisk the tomato paste with ¼ cup / 60 mL warm water in a small bowl, adding a spoonful of water at a time until the paste is completely diluted. Pour this into the pot.

Cover the pot, place it over high heat, and bring the liquid to a boil. Reduce the heat and simmer until the rolls are cooked through, and the rice, if using, is tender, about 45 minutes. Remove the plate and cool for 20 minutes or so before transferring the rolls from the pot to a serving platter. Serve them warm with a dollop of labneh.

Stuffing Three Ways

Lebanese cuisine has a devotion to stuffed foods of all kinds, from the humble grape leaf to the beautiful eggplant. The stuffing variations are as flexible as your own taste and imagination dictate. Here are three stuffings that you can use interchangeably with cabbage, grape leaves, and koosa.

Lamb and Rice Stuffing

This is the most traditional stuffing for cabbage, grape leaves, and koosa, and our family favorite, fragrant with cinnamon and enriched with melted butter. The medium-grain rice is especially nice here, imparting more tenderness than longer grain and melding perfectly with the meat.

Makes about 1 pound

- 1 cup / 190 g medium-grain rice
- 4 ounces (½ cup) / 60 g salted butter, melted
- 1 tablespoon kosher salt
- ¼ teaspoon freshly ground black pepper
- ½ teaspoon ground cinnamon
- 1 pound / 450 g ground lamb or beef (80 percent lean)

In a medium bowl, combine the rice, melted butter, salt, pepper, and cinnamon. Add the meat to the rice and mix well with your hands to combine everything thoroughly. At this point you can use the filling for any of the stuffed vegetable recipes.

Bulgur or Rice Stuffing with Parsley, Onion, and Tomato

Some classic Lebanese recipes call for straight-up tabbouleh as a stuffing for grape leaves and cabbage rolls; this is not quite so heavy on the herbs, but has a similar flavor. Add a cup / 150 g of cooked chickpeas to the mix for another variation.

Makes about 3 cups / 510 g

- 1 cup / 190 g fine grade bulgur (#1 grade) or medium-grain rice
- 1 small sweet onion, finely diced
- 2 scallions, finely chopped
- 2 large ripe tomatoes, seeded and finely diced
- ½ cup / 4 g fresh flat-leaf parsley leaves, finely chopped
- ¼ teaspoon ground cinnamon
- 2 teaspoons kosher salt
- Few grinds of black pepper
- ¾ cup / 180 mL neutral oil, such as canola or safflower

In a medium bowl, rinse the bulgur or rice with plenty of cool water, and pour off the water. Add all of the remaining ingredients and stir to combine them completely. At this point you can use the filling for any of the stuffed vegetable recipes.

Grape Leaves with Lemon

Whether you use fresh or jarred grape leaves, the method is the same—except the fresh leaves are soaked in hot water to soften them and the jarred ones in cold to remove the brine. To make smaller rolls, cut the larger leaves in half. The quantity of leaves here may seem huge, but it is traditional and typical to make a big pot of grape leaves, because they get eaten up in the blink of an eye. Once you get rolling, and if you corral others to help, it's fast and fun (of course, it's no problem to make a smaller quantity by halving the recipe). Grape leaves can be prepared ahead by rolling them, placing them in their cooking pot, and then freezing. Or, flash freeze the rolls on a parchment-lined sheet pan, transfer them to an airtight container, and freeze. Cook the frozen rolls in the pot they were frozen in, or if flash frozen, add to a pot lined with one of the meat bone options (if using) and a leaf or two. Cover with the chicken stock, and proceed. The stuffed grape leaves are meltingly tender and delicious the second day (and beyond) after cooking them.

Makes 80 to 100 grape leaf rolls

80 to 100 grape leaves, medium size, fresh or from a large jar

2 lamb or pork neck bones or ribs, 2 bone-in pork chops, or 6 chicken wings (optional)

1 recipe Lamb, Bulgur, or Rice stuffing (page 89)

2 lemons

4 cups / 950 mL chicken stock, vegetable stock, or water, plus more as needed

2 teaspoons kosher salt

Labneh (page 29), for serving

Rinse the leaves thoroughly. Soak jarred leaves in cold water, or fresh leaves in hot water, for 15 minutes. Prepare a deep pot with a lid by lining the bottom with the pieces of meat, which will impart great flavor to the rolls. Spread 3 large leaves over the top of the meat, or line the bottom of the pot with the leaves if you're not using the meat.

Place as many of the grape leaves facing vein-side up as will fit on a large work surface. The wider, stem-end of the leaf should be toward you. Trim each stem completely from each leaf, taking care not to cut into the leaf itself. Drop a heaping teaspoon of filling across that stem edge of the leaf. Shape it into a long finger, leaving enough leaf on either side of the stuffing to tuck the sides of the leaf in. Fold each side, right and left, of the leaf over the meat like an envelope, and then roll from the center, securely, away from you. Repeat with all of the leaves and filling.

Arrange the stuffed leaves, seam-side down, in rows in the prepared pot. Alternate the direction of the rows with each layer of stuffed leaves in the pot. Slice one of the lemons into ¼-inch / .5 cm slices and lay them on top of the rolls. Top them with a salad plate face-down over the top of the rolls, to hold them down while they cook.

Fill the pot with chicken stock, vegetable stock, or water up to the plate. Add the salt to the cooking liquid. Cover and bring slowly to a boil. After about 20 minutes, squeeze the juice of the remaining lemon into the broth. Reduce the heat to low and simmer for about 30 minutes longer, or until the rice is tender when you bite into a roll. Remove the plate and allow the grape leaves to cool for 20 minutes before removing them from the pot.

Serve the stuffed grape leaves with the cooked lemon slices as a garnish, along with some labneh as a dip or sauce. They are delicious hot, warm, or room temperature.

How to identify, clean, and store fresh grape leaves

One of the first, and favorite, things I ever wrote about food was a poem about picking grape leaves. There is, it seems, poetry to be found in the memory of being a child following the ladies out to the edge of a parking lot somewhere to pick what felt like illicit leaves, to be stuffed for our big pots of grape leaf rolls.

Every spring, when the vines have unfurled their leaves at that perfect moment between tender and strong, I imagine the mass exodus of Lebanese coming out of their homes across the wide world and scurrying out to their secret vines to pick the leaves by the hundreds, even thousands. It's our pot of gold at the end of the rainbow, our summer season's greeting, our heart's content. Our grape leaf.

Often we have to turn to jars of leaves for our rolls, but fresh leaves are a tradition worth holding onto. Mothers teach their children and then their grandchildren, and then we teach ours this:

Generally grape leaves are picked from wild vines. Vines cultivated for grapes are not used for their leaves, because they are not tender or as flavorful. The wild vines are just that, wildly giving all of their energies over to the leaves and never bearing fruit. The vines are not as a rule planted in the gardens of the Lebanese in the U.S. (though I vow to have one of my own someday, and to grow starters for all of you), at least not around here. In the Lebanese villages I've visited, every home has a beautiful, grape-leaf laden trellis gracing a front or back patio. Now that's living! Here I think we must enjoy the thrill of the chase to find the leaves along fences in remote and unsuspecting places. When we pick there, a passerby wonders what an odd thing it is we're doing.

Wild grape leaves have three lobes and are notched all the way around. The vine itself is reddish and the leaves are bright green.

Pick the medium-sized leaves. They are tenderer than the larger leaves, but stronger than the very small leaves and will hold more stuffing. Pick at the base of the stem, where it attaches to the vine. That stem will be trimmed off later, but it protects the leaf from tearing when picked and gives the leaf more longevity until it's used.

Ignore the leaves that have holes or tears in them. They're useless for stuffing.

Store the leaves by freezing them, without washing them, in stacks wrapped well with plastic wrap, and then placed in heavy-duty freezer bags. Aunt Hilda froze hers in a shoe box for reinforcement. Smart. This protects the leaves from the cold and from being banged around by other things in the freezer. If you're holding the leaves for just a few days, keep them in a ventilated bag in the refrigerator.

Frozen leaves last 6 months to a year in the freezer. I've used year-old frozen leaves, and they were a little dry and some frost-bitten, but they rolled and cooked up beautifully. And tasted wonderful.

Stuffed Koosa in Tomato Broth

Coring the koosa is simple and fun once you get the hang of it. The scrapings are not to be wasted; they're delicious in a Lebanese-style omelet with herbs (page 127).

Makes about 8 servings

- 18 pale green koosa (substitute small 5-inch / 13 cm zucchini and/or yellow squash)
- 1 recipe Lamb, Bulgur, or Rice Stuffing (page 89)
- 1 (28-ounce / 795 g) can tomato puree or tomato sauce
- ½ teaspoon kosher salt, plus more as needed

- Few grinds of black pepper
- 6 large garlic cloves, peeled and halved
- 1 medium yellow onion, quartered
- 1 bay leaf
- Labneh (page 29), for serving

Cut the stems from each squash. If your squash is bent at the neck, cut below the bend so you have a straight shot for coring and stuffing.

Insert the corer into the cut end of the squash as far as it will go without puncturing the other end, and twist. Pull out the core. Do this numerous times, scraping against the sides of the squash with gentle pressure until you've hollowed it out, leaving about ⅛ inch / 3 mm all the way around. If you do puncture a squash, it's still useable. Just eat that one, the ugly duckling, yourself as a treat for having worked hard on your koosa.

Fill each koosa with the stuffing by hand, pushing it in so that there aren't any air pockets. The rice or bulgur needs room to expand when it cooks, so leave about ¼ inch / .5 cm of space at the opening of the koosa. If you're using the meat stuffing, form any leftover stuffing into meatballs.

In a stockpot, season the tomato puree or sauce with the salt and pepper. Place the koosa upright in the pot with the stuffed end facing up, leaning the squash on an angle against one another so it won't

take as much liquid to cover them completely. Tuck in the garlic cloves, onion quarters, and bay leaf (and arrange the meatballs on top of the koosa, if using). Pour in enough water so that the koosa (and meatballs) are just covered. Cover the pot and bring the liquid to a boil over medium-high heat. Reduce the heat to medium-low and simmer until the squash is tender and the filling is cooked through, about 50 minutes. Add another cup or two / 240 to 475 mL of water and a pinch of salt if the broth looks like it is getting too thick.

Cool the koosa for about 20 minutes. Gently remove them from the pot using tongs or a big spoon into a serving bowl or individual bowls or plates. Taste the tomato broth, which is now a bit thicker and sauce-like, and adjust the seasonings, adding salt and pepper as needed.

Serve the koosa with the broth spooned over it. You can also make a cut down the length of the koosa with the side of a spoon and ladle the broth over that, to moisten the stuffing. Top the koosa with a dollop of labneh and serve it warm.

A Note about Koosa

Lebanese *koosa* (also spelled *cusa, kusa, kousa, coosa,* or *cousa*) is a small, pale green summer squash that is becoming more readily available at grocery stores and farmers' markets. Koosa is sometimes called Korean squash, grey squash, or Tatume squash. We have a special tool just for coring koosa, a long, narrow metal corer or pick, similar to a zucchini corer but longer and narrower. Find the Lebanese koosa corer in Middle Eastern markets or online (see page 243), or use a standard zucchini corer. Koosa can be cored and frozen in an airtight container or freezer bag, then thawed, stuffed, and cooked as directed.

ARE YOU A KOOSA?

Many of us at some point or another have called a small child "pumpkin." Sweet little thing you just want to eat up. My father was someone who enjoyed taking liberties with language (one of his life's missions was to know the English language brilliantly, perhaps to get back at the guys behind the meat counter whom he'd witnessed, as a child, teasing his mother's broken English), and he developed his own kind of Arabic/English comedian-language that needed no translation to make sense to everyone in our family. I honestly don't know if it's commonly used or if Dad coined it himself when he started calling his children "koosa." Sweet summer squash you just want to eat up.

He was a Lebanese father through and through, which meant that his children were his children no matter their age. This fact, along with my petite stature, caused me in my early 20s to work extra hard to be regarded as a Professional Woman, all grown up in suits and heels. But in a moment, in a flash, my father could pull back the curtain and reveal that I was not the Wizard of Oz, but still, on some level, his little girl.

I was working my first real job for an association in Lansing, Michigan. I sat in an open office area where we could all hear each other's conversations. One sunny morning my dad came through the front door for a meeting he had in the building, peeked his head around the corner to find me at my desk, and boomed, "HOW'S MY KOOSA?!"

I cringed. Hey, I was The Director of Communications.

But that look on his face, and that he expressed his love so freely—that's the kind of memory that you pull out of your back pocket like a well-worn St. Jude prayer card, a solace in desperate times.

Now we always ask the delicious little children in the family: "Are you a koosa?!" And they laugh and smile, and know exactly what we mean.

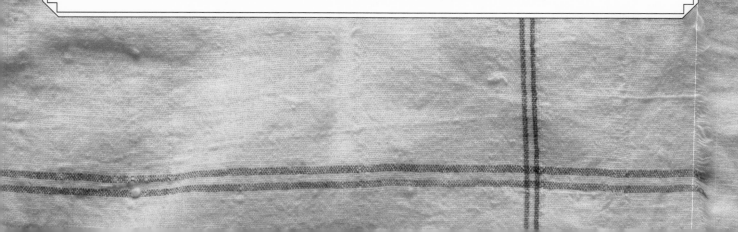

Stuffed Koosa with Yogurt and Mint

Koosa poached in minted yogurt is a sumptuous classic and always a treat. The cornstarch prevents the yogurt from curdling with the heat, as does using whole milk yogurt.

Makes about 8 servings

- 18 pale green koosa (substitute small 5-inch / 13 cm zucchini and/or yellow squash)
- 1 recipe Lamb, Bulgur, or Rice Stuffing (page 89)
- 6 cups / 1.5 kg plain, unsweetened whole milk yogurt or laban (page 26)
- 1 garlic clove, minced

- 1 tablespoon crushed dried mint, plus more for serving
- 1 tablespoon kosher salt
- 2 tablespoons cornstarch
- ¼ cup / 60 mL cold water

Cut the stems from each squash. If your squash is bent at the neck, cut below the bend so you have a straight shot for coring and stuffing.

Insert the corer into the cut end of the squash as far as it will go without puncturing the other end, and twist. Pull out the core. Do this numerous times, scraping against the sides of the squash with gentle pressure until you've hollowed it out, leaving about ⅛ inch / 3 mm all the way around. If you do puncture a squash, don't throw it away in a huff! It's still useable. Just serve that one, the ugly duckling, to yourself as a snack before dinner, your treat for having worked hard on your koosa.

Fill each koosa with the stuffing by hand, pushing it in so that there aren't any air pockets. The rice or bulgur needs room to expand when it cooks, so leave about ¼ inch / .5 cm of space at the opening of the koosa. If you're using the meat stuffing, form any leftover stuffing into meatballs.

Arrange the stuffed koosa, cut-end facing up, in a stockpot. Sprinkle with 1 tablespoon of the salt, and then cover them with 3 quarts / 3 L of water. Bring the water to a boil over high heat, and then reduce the heat to medium and simmer until the koosa is partially cooked through, about 20 minutes.

In another stockpot, heat the yogurt or laban, garlic, mint, and salt over medium heat. In a small bowl, combine the cornstarch with the cold water. Stir the cornstarch mixture into the yogurt mixture and bring the yogurt just to a boil over medium heat, stirring constantly until the yogurt is slightly thickened.

Using tongs, transfer the par-cooked koosa from the cooking water to the pot with yogurt, discarding the cooking water. Return the yogurt just to a boil, and then reduce the heat and simmer, uncovered, until the koosa is cooked through, about 15 minutes.

Spoon the koosa and yogurt into individual bowls and serve it immediately, dusted with more crushed dried mint.

Eggplant with Lamb, Tomato, and Pine Nuts

Sheik al Mehsheh, a meal "fit for a king," is one of the most delectable ways to prepare eggplant. Traditionally, small eggplant are halved and stuffed with the lamb filling, then baked in tomato sauce. My mother's version is this layered style, which gives the eggplant a deeply caramelized flavor. She always made eggplant as the ultimate homecoming dish for any of her five children coming home from college, and then from our various cities across the country. Nothing could make us more overjoyed than walking into the house to the scent of sheik al mehsheh, except for a mother's warm embrace.

Makes 8 servings

2 large, firm eggplants

4 tablespoons extra-virgin olive oil, divided

2 teaspoons kosher salt, divided

1 medium-size yellow onion, finely diced

2 garlic cloves, minced

1 pound / 450 g ground lamb or beef (80 percent lean)

½ teaspoon ground cinnamon

Several grinds of black pepper

1 (28-ounce / 795 g) can tomato sauce

½ cup / 75 g Butter Toasted Pine Nuts (page 33)

1½ cups / 360 mL warm water

12 ounces / 340 g fresh mozzarella cheese

1 recipe Lebanese Vermicelli Rice (page 147)

Preheat the broiler and line a baking sheet with foil or parchment. Trim the stem from each eggplant, and without peeling them, cut the eggplants in ½-inch / 1.5 cm slices. Brush both sides of the eggplant slices with 2 tablespoons of the olive oil, and sprinkle them with 1 teaspoon of the salt. Arrange the slices on the prepared baking sheet and broil them in batches until they are deep mahogany brown (they'll be slightly charred in some spots), turning them once to brown both sides, 10 to 15 minutes total.

Adjust the oven to 375°F / 190°C with a rack positioned in the center.

In a medium sauté pan, heat 1 tablespoon of the remaining olive oil over medium heat. Add the chopped onion and sauté it until it is translucent, but not browned, stirring occasionally. Stir in the garlic and cook just until it is fragrant, about a minute. Add the ground lamb or beef, breaking up the meat into very small pieces with the side of a metal spoon, stirring frequently. Season the mixture with a teaspoon of the salt, the cinnamon, and the pepper. Sauté until the meat is just cooked through, continuing to break up the meat into small pieces as it cooks.

Coat a 13 x 9 x 2-inch / 33 x 23 x 5 cm baking or similar sized gratin dish with a tablespoon of olive oil. Spread about ½ cup / 120 mL of tomato sauce in the bottom of the dish. Lay several eggplant slices in a single layer over the sauce, covering as much surface area of the bottom of the dish as possible. Spoon half of the meat evenly over the eggplant and pour half of the remaining tomato sauce evenly over the meat. Sprinkle with one-third of the pine nuts. Now layer again with eggplant, meat, pine nuts, and tomato sauce. Finish with a layer of eggplant and cover that with more tomato sauce, sprinkling the top with pine nuts.

Pour the warm water around the perimeter of the eggplant. This is an important step, or your sauce will be too thick; it may seem watery at first when you do this but the sauce will thicken as it bakes.

Cover the pan tightly with foil and bake it for 90 minutes. Remove the foil and top the eggplant evenly with fresh mozzarella cheese (rub the soft cheese between your fingers to break it up into small pieces). Bake for about 15 minutes longer, uncovered, until the cheese is bubbling and golden. Serve the eggplant warm, over rice.

A Note about Kibbeh

Kibbeh in all of its forms—raw, baked, fried, stuffed, and vegetarian—is one of the defining dishes of Lebanese cuisine. Kibbeh is a mixture of bulgur wheat with other ingredients, most classically lamb, fragrantly spiced and eaten for meals from celebratory to casual. Whenever people who aren't Lebanese eat our raw kibbeh, *kibbeh nayeh*, with relish, we consider them an honorary Lebanese, "one of the family." But it's always exciting to share kibbeh in its many other delicious iterations, some with no meat at all.

When procuring meat for kibbeh, especially for raw kibbeh, keep these tips in mind:

Kibbeh is excellent made with quality lamb or beef, though leg of lamb is traditional. The best cuts of beef are ultra-lean cuts of top round, eye of round, or sirloin tip. Though beef tenderloin is very lean, it is too soft for kibbeh and becomes mushy. Ideally, find grass-fed beef or leg of lamb raised on a family farm.

Never use ground meat that has not been specially ground for kibbeh, whether at home or by the butcher, and never use meat from the display case at the market. This meat is not safe to eat raw, nor is it lean or clean enough for any kind of kibbeh.

Purchase and grind your meat the same day you will eat it. Ideally you'll grind the meat yourself, but if the butcher will grind the meat, tell him or her that you are making Lebanese kibbeh and it is meant to be eaten raw (the grind is also the same if you are going to bake or fry it). Instruct the butcher (because this isn't negotiable and it's a point worth making every time) to grind on sterile blades, which is typically first thing in the morning (so plan ahead when ordering), and to trim all fat and gristle from the meat before grinding.

Raw kibbeh meat can be frozen. Pack it thinly in airtight containers so it thaws more readily. Be sure to thaw kibbeh meat in the refrigerator for one day, and then make and eat the raw kibbeh immediately.

You may notice that the interior of your freshly ground, packaged kibbeh meat is bright reddish-pink with a purple-gray interior. This is due to a pigment in meat that is naturally purple-gray. When the meat is exposed to oxygen, it turns red. Break up the meat, and the gray interior meat will turn pink after about 15 minutes of exposure to the air.

Raw Kibbeh (Kibbeh Nayeh) with Househ, page 102

Raw Kibbeh (Kibbeh Nayeh) with Househ

The meat for raw kibbeh must be handled with care; see the notes about raw meat for kibbeh (page 100). It's traditional to eat kibbeh topped with househ, ground beef or lamb sautéed with onions and finished with toasted pine nuts and a squeeze of lemon. Serve the lemony househ in its own bowl alongside, and everyone can scoop a big spoonful over the kibbeh on their plates. A small plate of raw kibbeh also makes a wonderful maza, as an appetizer dish.

Makes 4 to 6 servings

For the kibbeh:

1 cup / 190 g fine bulgur (#1 grade)

1 pound / 450 g leg of lamb or eye of round beef, trimmed of all fat and gristle

1 to 2 tablespoons kosher salt

Freshly ground black pepper, to taste (about 5 grinds)

1 medium-size sweet onion, half coarsely chopped and half finely chopped, for serving

1 cup / 240 mL ice water

2 teaspoons ground cinnamon

¼ teaspoon cayenne pepper

2 to 3 tablespoons extra-virgin olive oil, for serving

5 leaves fresh mint, finely chopped

1 tablespoon Butter Toasted Pine Nuts (page 33)

For the househ:

1 tablespoon extra-virgin olive oil

1 medium-size yellow onion, diced

1 pound / 450 g ground lamb or beef chuck

½ teaspoon ground cinnamon

1 teaspoon kosher salt

Few grinds of black pepper

Juice of 1 lemon

2 tablespoons toasted pine nuts

Rinse the bulgur twice in a small bowl, letting the bulgur settle for a few seconds before pouring off the water. Add enough fresh water just to cover the bulgur, about 2 cups. Soak it for 30 minutes, or until the bulgur is softened. Either ask a trusted butcher to grind the trimmed meat for you (twice on sterile blades), or grind it yourself. To grind the meat, slice the trimmed meat into pieces, about 4 x 2 inches / 10 x 5 cm. Season lightly with salt and pepper and freeze the meat on a parchment-lined sheet pan for 30 minutes. Grind the meat twice through the grinder attachment's large holes.

Puree the coarsely chopped sweet onion in the food processor or blender (a tablespoon of cold water can be added to keep the blender moving with the onion).

To mix the kibbeh, think of it as a dough that is kneaded. Place the ice water in a small bowl: you will use it to keep your just-washed hands wet and cold, and to add water a little at a time to the kibbeh as you knead. Pour off and squeeze out as much remaining water from the bulgur as possible. In a large bowl, knead the meat with the pureed onion and about half of the bulgur. Dip your hands in the ice water a few times as you knead, using them to add about 3 tablespoons of the water to the kibbeh in total; be careful not to add too much water to the kibbeh or it will become mushy. Add the remaining bulgur and knead until it's fully incorporated. Season the kibbeh with salt, pepper, cinnamon, and cayenne, kneading everything together and tasting and adjusting the seasoning as needed. The kibbeh is ready when you taste it and want to keep eating more. If you are not eating the kibbeh raw, you can taste it by frying a small spoonful of the kibbeh in a touch of olive oil in a small skillet.

To serve, flatten the kibbeh on a platter to about an inch thickness, and smooth the top and sides with your hand dipped in the ice water. My mother, like her mother, always makes the sign of the cross in the top of her kibbeh and garnishes with fresh mint; another traditional way is to score the top of the kibbeh with the tip of an overturned spoon, making ridges in rows. Drizzle the kibbeh with olive oil and garnish it by arranging the finely chopped sweet onion, mint, and pine nuts in the center.

To make the househ accompaniment, heat the olive oil in a medium skillet over medium-low heat. Sauté the diced yellow onion until it is soft and translucent but not browned, about 10 minutes. Add the ground meat and season it with cinnamon, salt, and pepper. Cook the meat until it is browned, breaking it up into small pieces with the side of a large metal spoon as it cooks. Squeeze the lemon (seeds removed) over the meat, and stir in the toasted pine nuts.

Serve the househ in a bowl alongside the platter of kibbeh, to be spooned over the top of the kibbeh as it is served on each plate.

Baked Kibbeh Sahnieh

Kibbeh dishes make such outstanding use of meat by stuffing the meat with yet more meat that I've wondered more than once what about our culinary history led us to this beloved combination, this meat bonanza. All I can say is that when you are cooking with exceptional ingredients such as the perfectly lean, nearly sweet meat used for kibbeh, you just can't get enough. I also have the idea that these dishes represent a kind of strength. It's something like what my Sitto used to tell me about the farm she grew up on, where not one thing was wasted when it came to cooking and keeping house. So my thought is that kibbeh was probably served infrequently and specially in the rather humble Lebanese mountain villages where my family comes from, so when they indulged, they indulged big. And what could be bigger than serving meat with the meat? Here the kibbeh is made into a layered casserole called *sahnieh*, stuffed with the househ, and topped with pats of butter to give the lean meat some moisture and richness. The sahnieh is delicious topped with labneh or hummus, and eaten with flatbread or pita bread.

Makes 8 servings

1 tablespoon extra-virgin olive oil

1 cup / 240 mL ice water

1 recipe Raw Kibbeh with Househ (page 102)

2 tablespoons cold salted butter

Preheat the oven to 400°F / 200°C and place one of the racks in the center.

Coat an 8-inch / 20 cm square baking dish with the olive oil. Set up a small bowl with the ice water where you are working and coat your hands with the water as you flatten and shape the kibbeh. Use half of the kibbeh to form a flat layer covering the bottom of the baking dish; it is easiest to do this in ¼-cup / 43 g portions of kibbeh, flattened between your palms and pressed into the bottom of the pan, smoothing any seams as you add each portion. The layer should be about ½ inch / 1.5 cm thick. Smooth the top of the layer with cold water.

Spread the househ evenly over the flat kibbeh layer. Using the remaining kibbeh meat, form another flat ½-inch- / 1.5 cm thick layer in the same manner as the bottom layer over the househ. Press this layer in gently against the filling, and smooth the top with a sprinkling of cold water.

Cut squares into the kibbeh before baking it by scoring through to the center househ layer but not all the way to the bottom of the dish, in three rows (two cuts) in each direction of the pan. Score, but don't cut through, each square diagonally as well (both ways, to form an X over each square) for a traditional, decorative top.

Place a dab of butter on each square—this adds a wonderful, savory flavor as well as moisture to the kibbeh, and encourages a dark brown crust on top. Bake the kibbeh for about 50 minutes, or until it is deep golden brown. Be sure to let the kibbeh bake long enough to get crusty on top; place the kibbeh under the broiler to encourage browning, if needed. There may be some juice around the perimeter of the kibbeh; this will reabsorb into the kibbeh, but before that happens, immediately after the sahnieh is removed from the oven, dip a pastry brush into the juices along the sides of the kibbeh and brush it liberally over the top.

Cool the kibbeh slightly, and then cut into the scored squares (an X will remain on top of each square) to serve. The kibbeh may want to fall apart; serve it carefully and push it back together into layers on the plates or serving platter, if needed.

Main Dishes

Fried Kibbeh with Mint Butter

I was absolutely dazzled when my sister-in-law Silvia's mother, Blanca, made her fried kibbeh balls stuffed with butter flecked with mint rather than the traditional househ for us. It was so good that when I worked at Boulette's Larder in San Francisco after culinary school, I shared the dish with the chef. I jumped for joy when she put it on her incredibly high-end lunch menu and asked me to make it for her customers, along with my flatbread and her rich homemade labneh. The kibbeh is delicious fried, but it is also good baked on heavy sheet pans in a 400°F / 200°C oven for about 25 minutes. Brush the kibbeh balls first with olive oil or melted butter and bake until they are deep golden brown. To stuff the kibbeh balls with househ rather than mint butter, use the househ recipe on page 102. As with all kibbehs, a dollop of labneh is excellent with these.

Makes 6 main course servings

5 sprigs fresh mint leaves, divided

4 ounces / 120 g cold unsalted butter, cut into 1-inch / 2.5 cm pieces

Pinch of kosher salt

1 cup / 240 mL ice water

1 recipe Raw Kibbeh, without the househ (page 102)

Neutral oil, such as canola or safflower, for frying

In a food processor, pulse half of the mint leaves until they are finely chopped, stopping to scrape down the sides of the bowl as you go. Add the butter and salt, and pulse until everything is combined and the butter is slightly softened. Taste and add another pinch of salt if needed. If the butter is meltingly soft, chill it in the refrigerator for 10 minutes.

Keep the cup of ice water in a small bowl nearby. Thinking of the kibbeh as dough that is being shaped and stuffed, shape about 2 tablespoons of the kibbeh into a ball. Wet the palm of the hand the kibbeh is resting in with cold water, and use your first finger of the other, dominant hand to hollow out the ball of meat by pushing into it, but not completely through the other end. Press the walls of the ball with your finger to about ⅛-inch / 3 mm thick all the way around, to form a little oval cup-like shape about 2 inches / 5 cm long and 1½ inches / 4 cm across.

Using a demitasse spoon or other very small spoon, fill the kibbeh shell with mint butter. Be careful not to get the filling on the edge of the shell where it is going to seal, so that it will close seamlessly and stay closed. After inserting the filling, push the kibbeh together at the open end with your fingertips and gently shape the kibbeh into a torpedo by rolling it in the palms of your hands, using the tips of your fingers to pull each end out to a point. Smooth the kibbeh with a touch of ice water, making sure there aren't any fissures. Set the stuffed kibbeh aside on a parchment-lined sheet pan as you make them. Save the remaining butter for topping the finished kibbeh.

To fry the kibbeh, fill a large, heavy, cast iron or nonstick skillet with enough neutral oil to reach halfway up the sides, or at least 2 inches / 5 cm from the top. Heat the oil to 350°F / 175°C, or until a small piece of mint bubbles up right away when dropped in the oil. Working in batches, place several kibbeh balls gently into the oil, using a large slotted spoon to slide them in and leaving a bit of breathing room around each one. Fry them until they are deep golden brown, and then turn them over with tongs and fry the other side to deep golden brown, about 4 minutes total. If the kibbeh balls stick slightly to the bottom of the pan, use a metal spatula to gently scrape them from the pan. Remove the kibbeh from the pan with a slotted spoon or tongs, and place them on a paper towel-lined platter.

To serve, melt the remaining mint butter in a small skillet over medium heat, and drizzle that over the finished kibbeh. Lightly chop the remaining mint leaves and sprinkle them over the kibbeh as a garnish. Serve the fried kibbeh right away, as soon as they are cool enough to eat.

The fried kibbeh freezes well and will hold in the refrigerator for a couple of days. Reheat them in a 375°F / 190°C oven until warmed through.

Vegan Tomato Kibbeh

We tend to think of kibbeh dishes as having to do strictly with meat, but there is a tremendous Lebanese tradition of vegetarian kibbeh. While tomato kibbeh is at its finest at the height of tomato season, it tastes wonderful even with winter tomatoes. Serve the kibbeh with fattoush (page 84) or a romaine salad (page 80), labneh, pita bread, and olives.

Makes 8 servings

1½ cups / 285 g fine bulgur (#1 grade)

5 sprigs fresh flat-leaf parsley

2 sprigs fresh mint

1 medium-size sweet onion, coarsely chopped

2 large, ripe tomatoes (1 pound)

½ red bell pepper, seeded, cored, and coarsely chopped

1½ teaspoons kosher salt

Few grinds of black pepper

½ teaspoon ground cinnamon

¼ teaspoon cayenne pepper

2 teaspoons crushed dried mint (page 31)

Juice of 1 lemon

½ cup / 120 mL extra-virgin olive oil, plus more for garnish

Place the bulgur in a medium mixing bowl.

In a food processor, pulse the parsley and mint until they are finely chopped, but not pureed. Add the onion and continue pulsing until it is also finely chopped, stopping to scrape down the sides of the bowl. Use a rubber spatula to scrape the herb-onion mixture into the mixing bowl with the bulgur.

Halve the tomatoes through the stem end and use your fingers to pull out the seeds. Discard the seeds and coarsely chop the tomato.

Add the tomatoes and red bell pepper to the processor. Pulse a few times, until they are finely chopped but not liquid, stopping to scrape down the sides of the bowl. Scrape this mixture into the mixing bowl.

Knead together the bulgur, herb-onion mixture, and tomato mixture, seasoning with salt, pepper, cinnamon, cayenne, crushed dried mint, lemon juice, and olive oil. Let the kibbeh rest for about 1 hour at room temperature, so that the bulgur will soak up the juices and soften. Taste the kibbeh and adjust the seasonings. Serve the kibbeh by spreading it to about ½-inch / 1.5 cm thickness on a platter. Using the tip of an overturned spoon or the tines of a fork, decoratively score the top of the kibbeh by making ridges all over. Chill until you're ready to serve the kibbeh, and then drizzle generously with more olive oil, and serve.

Potato and Spinach Kibbeh with Garlicky Mint Yogurt Sauce

I've been asked what makes this a kibbeh and not just a good ol' potato casserole. The distinction is the inclusion of the bulgur, which, like in meat kibbehs, is used as a binding ingredient, helping to bake the potato into a golden crust.

Makes 8 servings

3 pounds / 1.5 kg russet or Idaho potatoes, peeled and cut into 2-inch / 5 cm disks

1 tablespoon plus 1½ teaspoons kosher salt, divided

½ cup / 90 g fine bulgur (#1 grade)

4 ounces / 120 g salted butter, divided

Few grinds of black pepper

½ teaspoon onion powder

3 to 4 tablespoons extra-virgin olive oil

1 small sweet onion, finely chopped

1 (10-ounce / 285 g) package chopped frozen spinach, thawed and drained

¼ teaspoon ground cinnamon

2 teaspoons crushed dried mint

1 cup / 150 g cooked chickpeas

Juice of 2 lemons

1 recipe Garlicky Mint Yogurt Sauce (page 35)

In a large pot, cover the potatoes completely with cool water and add 1 tablespoon of the salt. Cover and bring to a boil, being careful not to let the water boil over. Remove the cover and reduce the heat to medium, cooking the potatoes until they are soft and mashable, about 15 minutes.

Rinse the bulgur twice in a small bowl, letting the bulgur settle for a few seconds before pouring off the water. Add enough fresh water just to cover the bulgur. Soak it for 30 minutes, or until the bulgur is softened, and then drain and completely squeeze out any excess water. Preheat the oven to 400°F / 200°C.

Drain the potatoes, putting them back on low heat in the pot to steam off any residual water. Off the heat, mash the potatoes with 4 tablespoons of the butter and the softened bulgur, ½ teaspoon of the salt, some pepper, and the onion powder. Set aside to cool.

In a large skillet, heat 3 tablespoons of the olive oil over medium heat. Add the onion with ½ teaspoon salt, and cook them until they are soft and translucent, but not browned. Add the chopped spinach, season with another ½ teaspoon salt and some pepper, the cinnamon, and the dried mint, adding a tablespoon of olive oil if the mixture seems dry. Stir in the chickpeas and lemon juice; taste and adjust the seasonings until it tastes lemony and delicious.

Coat an 8-inch / 20 cm square baking dish with 1 tablespoon of the butter. Use half of the potato mixture to make a 1-inch- / 2.5 cm thick layer in the bottom of the dish. Spoon the spinach mixture evenly over the bottom layer of potato kibbeh. Top the spinach mixture with another layer of the potato kibbeh. It's easiest to make the top layer in sections, forming flat patties of the potato in your hands and laying them over the spinach, closing up any seams and smoothing the top. Melt the remaining butter and generously brush the top of the kibbeh with it, reserving some to brush the kibbeh when it comes out of the oven.

Bake the kibbeh until it is warmed through and the top is golden brown, about 30 minutes. To encourage browning, place the kibbeh under the broiler for a few minutes, if needed. Brush the remaining melted butter over the kibbeh, and then cut it into squares and serve the kibbeh warm, topped with the mint yogurt sauce (page 35).

Yogurt-Poached Kibbeh with Parsley-Garlic Oil

For this recipe, you use the kibbeh balls from the recipe for fried kibbeh, but instead of frying them, poach them in yogurt—a wonderful flavor combination Cornstarch prevents the yogurt from curdling with the heat, as does using whole milk yogurt.

Makes 6 main course servings

6 cups plain, unsweetened whole milk yogurt or laban (page 26)

2½ tablespoons cornstarch

3 tablespoons cold water

1½ tablespoons crushed dried mint

1 teaspoon kosher salt, plus more to taste

1 tablespoon fresh lemon juice

1 recipe uncooked Fried Kibbeh with Mint Butter, at room temperature (page 106)

2 tablespoons extra-virgin olive oil

1 large garlic clove, minced

2 tablespoons fresh flat-leaf parsley, chopped

In a large heavy saucepan, begin to warm the yogurt or laban over medium heat.

In a small bowl, dissolve the cornstarch in the cold water. Whisk the cornstarch into the yogurt, along with the crushed dried mint, salt, and lemon juice.

Spoon the raw kibbeh balls into the yogurt, bring it to a boil, and then reduce the heat and simmer until the kibbeh are cooked through and the yogurt is slightly thickened, about 20 minutes.

While the kibbeh cooks, make the parsley-garlic oil. In a small skillet, warm the olive oil over medium-low heat. Add the garlic and cook just until it is fragrant and warm, about 1 minute. Add the parsley and a pinch of salt and warm that for 30 seconds. Remove the oil from the heat and set it aside until the kibbeh is finished cooking.

Serve the kibbeh in warmed soup bowls, four kibbeh in each bowl, along with a ladleful of the yogurt broth. Drizzle each with the parsley-garlic oil.

Spiced Lamb Kofta Burgers

Kofta is a super-flavorful meat-and-spice blend that is traditionally made by coating a skewer with the meat mixture. For ease, I like to make the kofta into burgers and eat them American-style. The size of the burgers can be standard burgers or smaller sliders; whatever the size, be sure to flatten them out as much as possible when shaping, so that they don't get too thick and puck-ish when they cook. The raw meat mixture becomes quite soft with all of the seasonings and onion, so it's helpful to chill it for a half hour or up to a day before grilling or broiling. Dress the burgers with Toum (page 30); a quickie alternative is purchased mayonnaise with some minced garlic stirred in. A topping of crumbled feta cheese is also delicious. To serve the kofta without buns, serve the patties over Lebanese Vermicelli Rice (page 147).

Makes 6 large burgers or 12 sliders

2 pounds / 900 g ground lamb

½ small yellow onion, grated

3 sprigs fresh flat-leaf parsley leaves, chopped

10 fresh mint leaves, chopped

2 teaspoons kosher salt

Several grinds of black pepper

1 teaspoon sumac

½ teaspoon ground cinnamon

2 tablespoons extra-virgin olive oil

6 hamburger buns, 12 slider buns, or pita bread, for serving

In a medium bowl, gently combine the lamb with the onion, parsley, mint, salt, pepper, sumac, and cinnamon. (Overworked meat becomes tough.) Shape the mixture into 6 large or 12 small flat patties. Dip your hands in cold water if they become sticky. Place the patties onto a waxed paper-lined plate or sheet pan, and then cover them with another sheet of waxed paper and chill them for 30 minutes or up to one day.

To grill the burgers, heat the grill to medium-high heat. Brush the patties with olive oil. Grill about 4 minutes per side, or until cooked through. To broil the burgers, place them a few inches under the broiler on high, turning once until cooked through, about 15 minutes total. Serve the burgers on buns with condiments, or with pita bread.

Roasted Leg of Lamb with Black Cherry-Pomegranate Salsa

One of the most exciting cuts of meat to celebrate with is a bone-in leg of lamb. The presentation is so luscious on a big carving board or platter. Up in Michigan, we are always looking for new ways to eat our abundant cherries—dressed with pomegranate molasses and spooned over the lamb, they taste just as striking as they look, a perfect sweet and tangy balance to the rich meat.

Makes 8 servings

For the lamb:

5 to 7 pounds / 2.2 to 3.2 kg lamb leg, bone in

3 tablespoons extra-virgin olive oil

Kosher salt and freshly ground black pepper

6 garlic cloves, minced

For the salsa:

3 tablespoons pomegranate molasses

Juice of 1 lemon

3 tablespoons extra-virgin olive oil

Pinch of kosher salt

Few grinds of black pepper

1 quart / 560 g black sweet cherries, pitted and halved

¼ cup / 2 g coarsely chopped fresh flat-leaf parsley

¼ cup / 2 g coarsely chopped fresh mint

Recipe Continues On Next Page

Bring the lamb to room temperature for about an hour before roasting. Using kitchen twine, tie the leg crosswise 3 or 4 times, about 3 inches / 7.5 cm apart.

Place the lamb on a rack set in the bottom of a roasting pan and drizzle the olive oil evenly over the top. Rub the oil over the fat and the meat and season it liberally all over with salt and pepper.

Position a rack in the oven far enough below the broiler so that the meat is a few inches from the heat. Turn on the broiler to high and broil the lamb for about 5 minutes, or until the top of the lamb is caramelized and looks seared. Turn the lamb over with tongs and broil the opposite side in the same way.

Remove the lamb from the oven and flip it back to its original side up. Turn off the broiler and reposition the oven rack to the center of the oven. Heat the oven to 325°F / 165°C.

Coat the top of the lamb with the minced garlic, tent the lamb loosely with foil, and roast for 1 hour, or until the internal temperature reaches 135°F / 57°C on a meat thermometer; if taken out at this temperature, after the lamb rests it will be medium-rare to medium. Remove the lamb from the oven and let it rest for 15 to 30 minutes before snipping the twine off and then carving.

While the lamb rests, make the cherry salsa (it can also be made a day in advance). In a medium bowl, whisk together the pomegranate molasses, lemon juice, olive oil, salt, and pepper. Add the cherries and stir to coat them with the vinaigrette. Gently stir in the parsley and mint.

To carve the lamb, place it on a cutting board with the bone parallel to the board. Make perpendicular slices to the bone, angling straight down until the knife hits the bone. Cut the lamb off the bone by slicing through the bottom of the slices, keeping the knife along the bone.

Serve the sliced lamb on a platter with the salsa alongside or spooned over the slices.

Green Bean and Lamb Stew

My sister Peg loves to claim this *lubieh*, also called *yahneh* (pronounced LOO-bee-yeh and YUH-nee), or any stew at all, the pride and joy of her kitchen. She wants to make this so often that I start to protest. Then she points at me with a knowing nod as I smack my lips eating it every single time, no matter how often she puts it on the table. Serve the stew over the rice with flatbread and labneh.

Makes 12 servings

2 to 3 tablespoons extra-virgin olive oil, or as needed

3 pounds / 1.5 kg leg of lamb or shoulder, trimmed and cut into 1-inch / 2.5 cm pieces

3 tablespoons kosher salt, divided

Several grinds of black pepper

8 ounces / 230 g button or baby bella mushrooms, cleaned and halved

1 medium-size yellow onion, finely diced

1 teaspoon ground cinnamon

2 (28-ounce / 825 mL) cans tomato sauce

3½ cups / 825 mL warm water (hint: use the tomato sauce can!)

1 cinnamon stick

1 pound / 450 g green beans, washed and trimmed

Lebanese Vermicelli Rice (page 147)

In a 6- to 8-quart / 6 to 7.5 L pot heat 2 tablespoons of the oil over medium-high heat. Pat the meat dry and season liberally with 1 tablespoon of the salt and 1 teaspoon of the pepper. Brown and caramelize the meat in batches over medium heat, leaving plenty of breathing room between the pieces of meat as it cooks (so that it will caramelize rather than steam), about 3 minutes per batch. Transfer the meat with tongs to a plate as each batch is finished.

Over medium-high heat, add the mushrooms to the pot with another tablespoon of oil if the pot seems dry. Season the mushrooms lightly with salt and pepper. Sauté the mushrooms until they are slightly caramelized and soft, scraping up the fond, or browned bits, from the bottom of the pan, 3 to 5 minutes.

Add the onion, season lightly with salt and pepper, reduce the heat to medium, and sauté until they are soft and translucent, 5 minutes.

Return the meat to the pot and stir in the ground cinnamon, tomato sauce, and water. Add the cinnamon stick and cover, bring to a boil, and then reduce to a simmer and cook for 90 minutes.

Stir in the green beans and cook, uncovered, until the beans are tender, about 15 minutes. Serve the stew piping hot over the vermicelli rice, which soaks up the juices nicely.

Grilled Lamb Skewers with Fresh Mint Sauce

The key to proper grilling of most any meat is to bring it to room temperature for up to two hours before cooking. This ensures even cooking and prevents the exterior of the meat from burning before the interior is cooked. The skewers can also be cooked under a high broiler in the oven. If you're using wooden skewers, soak them in water for 15 minutes before cooking with them so that they don't burn before the meat is ready. This shish kebab, also known as *laham meshweh*, is a family favorite in the summer, or in the winter, made by sautéing the lamb and onion sans skewers in a skillet on the stovetop.

Makes 8 (10-inch / 25 cm) skewers

2 pounds / 900 g leg of lamb, cut into 2-inch / 5 cm cubes

2 tablespoons kosher salt

Few grinds of black pepper

1 large red onion, cut into 2-inch / 5 cm cubes

⅓ cup / 80 mL extra-virgin olive oil

1 tablespoon granulated sugar

3 tablespoons sherry vinegar

1 small shallot, finely chopped

1 cup / 8 g fresh mint leaves, finely chopped

Place the meat on a parchment-lined sheet pan, season it generously all over with salt and pepper, and then set it aside to come to room temperature.

Heat a gas or charcoal grill to medium-high heat. Thread the skewers, preferably stainless steel, with a pattern of 2 pieces of meat, then 1 chunk of onion, repeated, leaving a bit of space between all of the pieces (about ⅛ inch / 3 mm).

Brush the meat and vegetables with olive oil. Place on the grill; for medium-rare meat, cook for 10 minutes with the lid down, and then flip with tongs and grill another 8 minutes, lid down.

Alternatively, cook the skewers on a broiler or sheet pan under a high broiler for about 30 minutes, turning them over halfway through cooking. Remove the skewers from the heat and let them rest for 10 minutes.

Remove the hot meat and onion from the skewers by pushing them off with a fork.

While the meat is resting, make the mint sauce by dissolving the sugar in the vinegar in a small bowl, and stirring in the shallot and mint. Serve alongside the grilled lamb.

Fragrant Chicken Soup with Vermicelli

The beauty of this soup is in its simplicity. The flavor of the chicken shines through and is complemented with fragrant cinnamon. You can use orzo instead of the vermicelli. Don't skimp on the fresh parsley before serving, as it contributes such an integral and lovely layer of fresh taste and color. A spoonful of labneh enriches a bowlful of the soup perfectly.

Makes 8 to 10 servings

One 3-pound / 1.35 kg free-range chicken, cut into parts, or 3 pounds / 1.35 bone-in breasts

1 large yellow onion, quartered

1 large carrot, peeled and cut into 2-inch / 5 cm pieces, plus 1 large carrot, finely chopped

1 celery stalk, cut into 2-inch / 5 cm pieces, plus 1 celery stalk, finely chopped

2 cinnamon sticks

6 whole peppercorns

1 tablespoon whole allspice berries

6 green cardamom pods

2 bay leaves

2 teaspoons kosher salt, plus more for seasoning

1 cup broken vermicelli noodles (approximately 1-inch / 2.5 cm pieces)

Juice of ½ lemon

Freshly ground black pepper, to taste (about 5 grinds)

Fresh flat-leaf parsley, coarsely chopped

In a large stock or soup pot, place the chicken, onion, 2-inch pieces of carrot and celery, cinnamon sticks, peppercorns, allspice, cardamom, and bay leaves with 2 teaspoons of the kosher salt. Cover the chicken by 2 inches / 5 cm with cold water. Bring just to a boil over high heat, but not a rolling boil (that will cloud the broth), and then reduce the heat to low (just hot enough to make slow, lazy bubbles). Skim the surface of the broth frequently with a spoon or skimming sieve to remove the foam.

Simmer the broth, uncovered, for about 45 minutes. Cut out the chicken breasts and set them aside if using a whole chicken, and continue cooking the rest of the chicken in the broth for another hour. (If you're using just chicken breasts, remove them and cool briefly, until you can handle them. Remove the meat and return the bones to the pot; continue cooking for 1 hour.) Remove all the remaining chicken and set it aside until it is cool enough to handle. Pour the broth through a fine mesh sieve or fine cheesecloth into another 3- or 4-quart / 3 or 4 L pot.

Remove the chicken from the bones and shred it and the breast meat finely into thin, 1-inch / 2.5 cm pieces. Add the finely chopped carrot and celery and the vermicelli to the strained broth and bring it to a simmer. Cook until the vegetables and pasta are tender, about 10 minutes. Add in the shredded chicken. Squeeze in the lemon juice and season the broth to taste with salt and pepper. Serve the soup in warmed bowls topped with the parsley.

Main Dishes

Yogurt Marinated Chicken Skewers with Toum Garlic Sauce

This is simply the most tender, succulent chicken you can eat—thanks to the yogurt marinade, which is a great tenderizer. These skewers are wonderful grilled, but broiling under high heat is delicious too. If you use wooden skewers, soak them in water for at least 15 minutes before using them, so that they don't burn before the chicken is cooked.

Makes 6 skewers

1 cup / 245 g plain, unsweetened whole milk yogurt or laban (page 26)

1 medium-size sweet onion, grated

3 garlic cloves, minced

Juice of ½ lemon

2 tablespoons crushed dried mint

3 tablespoons extra-virgin olive oil

4 skinless, boneless free-range chicken breast halves

1 teaspoon kosher salt, plus more as needed

Few grinds of black pepper

1 recipe Toum (page 30)

In a small bowl, combine the yogurt, onion, garlic, lemon, mint, and olive oil.

Cut the chicken into 1- to 2-inch / 2.5 to 5 cm pieces and place them in a medium bowl or a plastic ziplock bag. Pour the marinade over the chicken, cover the bowl or seal the bag, and refrigerate for at least 8 and up to 24 hours (the longer, the more flavorful).

Preheat a grill or broiler on medium-high.

Place the chicken in a colander and drain off the marinade. Pat the chicken dry with paper towels.

Thread 6 skewers with the chicken, leaving some breathing room (about ⅛ inch / 3 mm) between the pieces. Generously season the chicken all over with salt and pepper.

Grill the chicken over medium-high heat, or broil them on a broiler or sheet pan, until the chicken is cooked through and is slightly charred around the edges, about 10 minutes on the grill and about 20 minutes under the broiler. Turn the skewers over halfway through cooking.

Remove the cooked chicken from the skewers with a fork. Serve the chicken hot with the toum, either on the side for dipping or drizzled over the chicken after it has been removed from the skewers.

Hushweh
(Chicken Rice Pilaf with Butter Toasted Almonds)

Perhaps the most beloved Lebanese dish that my family has ever served anyone, *hushweh* (pronounced HUSH-wee) is one of the world's all-time great comfort foods. Its buttery goodness will bring peace and calm in the face of adversity, and will soothe a weary soul. Hushweh is also just plain quick and easy, a breeze to pull together on a busy evening. When time is tight, use a roasted chicken from the market. The chicken can be shredded in advance; bring it to room temperature before adding it to the rice mixture. This dish is excellent served with a romaine salad dressed with lemon vinaigrette (page 80), thin pita bread, labneh (page 29), and hummus (page 49).

Makes 12 servings

For the chicken:

1 (3- to 4-pound / 1.35 to 1.8 kg) free-range chicken

1 large yellow onion, quartered

2 tablespoons extra-virgin olive oil

½ teaspoon paprika

½ teaspoon granulated garlic powder

½ teaspoon kosher salt

Few grinds of black pepper

For the rice:

4 tablespoons salted butter

1 pound / 450 g ground beef chuck or lamb

½ teaspoon ground cinnamon

1 teaspoon kosher salt

Few grinds of black pepper

1 cup / 190 g parboiled long-grain white rice (such as Uncle Ben's)

2 cups / 475 mL chicken broth

1 cinnamon stick

¾ cup / 110 g Butter Toasted Almonds (page 33), divided

Heat the oven to 425°F / 220°C.

Pat the chicken dry. Place it in a large roasting pan. Stuff the cavity with the onion. Rub a couple of tablespoons of oil evenly over the skin and season the chicken all over lightly with paprika, garlic powder, salt, and pepper.

Roast the chicken until the juices run clear when the chicken is pierced and the meat reaches an internal temperature of 160°F / 70°C in the thigh on an instant-read thermometer, about 1 hour. Baste the chicken every 15 minutes with its juices while it roasts.

Melt 1 tablespoon of the butter in a 4-quart / 4 L Dutch oven or saucepan over medium heat. Add the ground beef and season it with the ground cinnamon, salt, and pepper. Cook the meat, stirring constantly and using a metal spoon to crumble it into small pieces until no trace of pink remains, about 5 minutes.

Stir the rice into the meat until it is completely coated with juices. Pour in the broth and bring it to a boil. Reduce the heat to low, tuck in the cinnamon stick, cover, and simmer for 20 minutes, or until all of the broth is absorbed.

Transfer the roasted chicken to a cutting board and when it is cool enough to handle, remove and discard the skin. Shred the chicken into 1-inch / 2.5 cm pieces.

Remove the cinnamon stick and add the chicken, ½ cup / 75 g of the toasted nuts, and the remaining 3 tablespoons butter to the hot rice mixture, stirring to combine. Taste and add more salt, if needed. Sprinkle with the remaining nuts and serve immediately.

Zucchini, Parsley, and Mint Omelets (Ijjeh)

I imagine this preparation for eggs came about when the bushels of koosa were cored, to be stuffed and cooked in tomato broth (page 93), and the Lebanese cook wanted to make good use, and something lovely, out of the piles of tender flesh that had been pulled from the centers of the squash. A grated zucchini does the trick nicely when we haven't made koosa recently but want our *ijjeh* (IJH-ee) anyway, eggs with fresh herbs and squash fried into little omelets. They make a delightful meal eaten with olives, tomato wedges, and flatbread, and work perfectly on the run cold, wrapped in a piece of pita or flatbread.

Makes 4 servings

1 large zucchini, grated (1 cup / 170 g)

1 teaspoon kosher salt, divided

4 tablespoons clarified butter (page 41), divided

2 scallions, white and green parts, very thinly sliced

4 large eggs

Few grinds of black pepper

2 tablespoons finely chopped fresh flat-leaf parsley

2 tablespoons finely chopped fresh mint

¼ cup / 30 g unbleached all-purpose flour

¼ cup / 60 g labneh (page 29), or substitute Greek yogurt

Pinch of granulated garlic powder

Drain the zucchini by salting it with ½ teaspoon of salt and placing it in a colander in the sink for 30 minutes. Squeeze the zucchini to remove more water.

Heat 1 tablespoon of the clarified butter in an 8-inch / 20 cm skillet over medium-high heat. Add the zucchini and scallions and cook them just until they are beginning to brown, about 3 minutes. Remove the zucchini and scallions from the skillet and place them on a plate to cool.

In a medium-sized bowl, whisk the eggs, remaining salt, pepper, parsley, and mint. Sprinkle the flour over the eggs 1 tablespoon at a time, slowly whisking it in. Stir in the scallions and zucchini.

Heat the remaining 3 tablespoons of clarified butter in a small nonstick skillet over medium heat. Ladle ⅓ cup / 60 g of the egg-zucchini mixture into the hot butter to make a single small omelet. Cook, spooning a bit of hot butter over the top of the omelet, for about 30 seconds, or until the edges of the omelet begin to turn golden and the top of the omelet is just starting to set. Flip the omelet over completely and cook for another 30 seconds. Place the omelet on a serving platter and continue cooking the rest of the omelets in the same way.

In a small bowl, whisk the labneh with the garlic powder.

Ijjeh tastes best once it's had a good 10 minutes to cool off, topped with the labneh.

Variation: Ijjeh with Koosa Scrapings

If you've made a big pot of stuffed koosa (page 93), then you've got the key ingredient for authentic *ijjeh*—the leftover cores of the squash that were scraped out to make way for the stuffing. Salt the squash scrapings with about a teaspoon of kosher salt, and drain them in a colander in the sink for about 30 minutes to remove some of the moisture. Squeeze them to remove still more moisture, and then chop the scrapings. Use them in place of the grated zucchini in the recipe for ijjeh, but without cooking the scrapings first. Just add them and the raw scallions to the egg mixture and continue from there. You will have a lot more than one cup of squash scrapings from a batch of koosa, and you can easily increase the ijjeh recipe to suit. Don't worry too much about having all of the amounts exact: your ijjeh will be delicious with more or less squash, and more or less scallion and herbs too. The scrapings will hold for a week in an airtight container or ziplock bag in the refrigerator.

Baked Eggs with Spinach, Labneh, and Sumac

One of my favorite projects in culinary school was our assignment to take a classic dish and make it new, make it ours, with a fresh approach. I always went for a Lebanese twist on the mostly classic French preparations we were learning, and kept the fun going at home when I was hard at work practicing techniques. I found our French baked eggs with cream to be one of the most divine things you can put in your mouth, second only to my Lebanese take on that dish, using seasoned labneh and topping everything with bright, tangy sumac.

Makes 4 servings

2 tablespoons salted butter, melted

Big handful of baby spinach leaves (about 16)

8 large eggs

⅓ cup / 80 g labneh (page 29), or substitute Greek yogurt

1 tablespoon grated sweet onion

½ teaspoon kosher salt

4 slices good bread for toast

Sumac, for garnish

Arrange a rack in the center of the oven and preheat the oven to 375°F / 190°C. Set a large kettle of water to boil.

Generously brush four 6-ounce / 180 g ramekins with some of the melted butter. Line the bottom of each dish with about 4 leaves of baby spinach in a single layer. Crack two eggs into each dish.

In a small bowl, whisk the labneh, onion, and salt with a tablespoon of water to make a sauce the consistency of heavy cream.

Spoon a couple of tablespoons of the labneh sauce over the egg white in each dish, avoiding the yolk so that it will stay a lovely bright yellow. Season each egg with a pinch of salt.

Place the ramekins in a 13 x 9 x 2-inch / 33 x 23 x 5 cm baking dish and place the dish in the oven on the center rack. Fill the pan with boiling water to reach halfway up the sides of the egg dishes, taking care not to get any water in the eggs. Bake the eggs for about 15 to 17 minutes, or until the whites are cooked and the yolks are still bright yellow and jiggle when shaken. Toward the end of the baking time, toast and butter the bread.

Remove the baking dish from the oven and carefully remove each ramekin from the hot water, drying the ramekins off. Drizzle the eggs with melted butter, and dust the eggs with sumac. Serve immediately, placing each hot ramekin on a plate, with buttered toast.

Olive Oil Fried Eggs with Za'atar

I learned this way with eggs from my husband, Dan. The first time I made him eggs, he asked where the za'atar was (yes, he's Lebanese too). He was as surprised that I had never put za'atar on my eggs as I was to hear that he always had. He was so proud that he taught me this that he started calling me "Za'atar" after that, a nickname I'll take any day. The za'atar makes these eggs special, but so does the olive oil they're fried in, which gives the eggs their crispy, lacey, golden edges. We always eat our fried eggs with tomato wedges, olives, and pita bread.

Makes 2 servings

2 tablespoons extra-virgin olive oil, divided

4 large eggs

Kosher salt and freshly ground black pepper, to taste

1 tablespoon za'atar

Heat a tablespoon of the olive oil in an 8-inch / 20 cm nonstick frying pan (with a lid that will fit over it) over medium heat until hot but not smoking.

Crack two eggs into the oil and cook until they are bubbling, becoming solid, and beginning to crisp around the edges. Be careful here because the oil can spatter and spew. Long sleeves help, as does a splatter screen.

Cover the pan briefly. Lift the lid every 30 seconds or so to release steam, cooking the yolk as far as you like it, about a minute for a runny yolk.

Transfer the eggs to a warm plate and drizzle them with some of the warm olive oil from the pan. Fry two more eggs this same way, adding another tablespoon of oil and heating that before cracking the eggs in.

Season the eggs with salt, pepper, and za'atar, and serve them warm.

Pan-Seared Snapper with Tahini Sauce and Toasted Pine Nuts

This wonderful dish is in every Lebanese cookbook I own. I had never tried it until recent years, and the discovery has made for a great addition to my fish repertoire. Typically the snapper is baked, but I think the delicious flavor that pan-frying imparts is even better. Fresh fish should always glisten, have little to no scent, and be firm to the touch. I never hesitate to ask when fish was delivered, and to smell a piece before I buy it. Frozen fish is a great option too, as it is ideally cleaned and flash-frozen right after it is caught. Look for vacuum-packed frozen fish, which protects the delicate flesh. For added kick, make the snapper spicy—the way it's traditionally served—by shaking some good hot sauce into the tahini sauce before serving.

Makes 4 servings

4 (4-ounce / 150 g) fillets red snapper, or 2 (8-ounce / 300 g) fillets halved crosswise

¼ teaspoon kosher salt

Few grinds of black pepper

Pinch of cayenne pepper

1 tablespoon salted butter

1 tablespoon extra-virgin olive oil

1 recipe Tahini-Yogurt Sauce (page 34)

¼ cup / 32 g Butter Toasted Pine Nuts (page 33)

Chopped fresh flat-leaf parsley, for serving

Season the snapper with salt, pepper, and cayenne. Bring the fish to room temperature, about ½ hour.

Heat a large heavy skillet over high heat for 1 minute. Once the pan is hot, reduce the heat to medium-high and add the butter and olive oil. When the butter foams up and is very hot (but not browned yet), lay the fillets in the pan. The fish should sizzle the moment it touches the pan. If they don't, remove them and wait for the pan to heat up.

Sauté the fillets until they are golden brown on one side, about 3 minutes, and then flip them over and sauté the second side until it is golden and the fish is opaque and flaky in the center, another 2 to 3 minutes.

Transfer the hot snapper to a warmed serving plate and drizzle the tahini sauce over the top. Sprinkle with the pine nuts and chopped parsley, and serve the fish immediately. If you are waiting more than 5 minutes to serve the fish, don't dress it with the tahini sauce until immediately before serving so that it doesn't dry out.

Pistachio-Crusted Whitefish with Parsley-Lemon Butter

Michigan is surrounded by the largest freshwater system in the world, the spectacular Great Lakes. The whitefish that comes from our cold, pristine waters is the darling of every table in Michigan, especially Up North. It's on menus at every restaurant and is turned out of most kitchens at home throughout the summer. Whitefish is tender, sweet, and light—a fish for even the most infrequent of fish-eaters. If whitefish is not available, any thin, white-fleshed fish will work well. This elegant, flavorful preparation is company-worthy.

Makes 4 servings

- 4 (4-ounce / 150 g) fillets whitefish, or 2 (8-ounce / 300 g) fillets halved crosswise
- 1¼ teaspoons kosher salt, divided
- Few grinds of black pepper
- ½ cup / 65 g unbleached all-purpose flour
- 2 large eggs
- ¾ cup / 110 g shelled roasted, salted pistachios, finely chopped
- Grated zest of 1 organic lemon, divided
- ½ cup / 4 g finely chopped fresh flat-leaf parsley, divided
- 2 tablespoons grapeseed, safflower, or canola oil
- 2 tablespoons salted butter
- Juice of ½ lemon

Season the whitefish fillets lightly with 1 teaspoon of salt and pepper and bring them to room temperature, about 30 minutes.

Prepare the coating by setting up three shallow bowls or rimmed plates. Whisk the flour in one bowl with a pinch of salt. Whisk the eggs in a second bowl with a pinch of salt. Combine the chopped pistachios, half of the lemon zest, and ¼ cup / 2 g of the chopped parsley in the third bowl.

Heat the oil in a large sauté pan over medium heat.

Just before sautéing, dip a fillet in the flour, and then the egg. Press the top of the fillet into the pistachio mixture, coating it evenly with nuts on one side. Repeat this with another fillet.

Reduce the heat to medium-low so that the nuts don't burn (they can, easily), and place two of the fillets pistachio-side down in the hot sauté pan. Sauté the fish until the pistachio coating is golden brown, about 3 minutes. Use a long metal spatula to flip the fish, and cook for another 4 minutes, or until it is golden and the fish is just cooked through.

Move the fish to a warm plate and tent the plate with foil to keep the fish warm while you coat and cook the remaining two fillets in the same manner as the first two.

In a small pan, melt the butter over medium-high heat. Add the lemon juice, the remaining lemon zest, parsley, and ¼ teaspoon salt, and cook for another 30 seconds or so. Drizzle the lemon butter over the fish and serve immediately.

Grains & Legumes

Garlicky Lentil Soup with
Swiss Chard and Lemon

Toasted Bulgur with Poached
Chicken and Cinnamon

Mujadara with Crispy Onions

Freekeh with Tomato
and Chickpeas

Fresh Herb Falafel with
Tahini-Yogurt Sauce

Fava Beans and Chickpeas
with Garlic, Lemon, and Olive Oil

Crunchy Roasted Za'atar Chickpeas

Lebanese Vermicelli Rice

Garlicky Lentil Soup with Swiss Chard and Lemon

You're going to be tempted to eat up the garlicky chard and onion sauté before it goes into the soup. And that's just fine because it tastes so delicious like that. But if it's soup you're after, just taste and then stir the fragrant mix into the lentils. This soup tastes best when it's not piping hot, but has cooled down for a few minutes so the flavors can really shine through. A classic *rushta* (Lebanese lentil soup) also contains cooked pasta noodles like linguine, which can easily be added to the recipe below. It is also fine to leave out the flour if you would like a gluten-free soup.

Makes 10 servings

½ cup / 95 g brown or green whole lentils

4 cups / 950 mL cool water

1 teaspoon kosher salt, divided

¼ cup / 60 mL extra-virgin olive oil

1 large yellow onion, finely diced

1 bunch Swiss chard, leaves and stems separated, cleaned, trimmed, and chopped into 1-inch pieces

¾ teaspoon ground coriander

Few grinds of black pepper

4 large garlic cloves, minced

¾ cup / 6 g fresh cilantro leaves, coarsely chopped, divided

1½ teaspoons unbleached all-purpose flour

Juice of ½ lemon

In a 4-quart / 4 L pot over high heat, bring the lentils, water, and ½ teaspoon of salt to a boil. Reduce the heat and simmer, covered, just until the lentils are tender, about 20 minutes.

Meanwhile, in a medium sauté pan, heat the olive oil over medium heat. Add the onion and chard stems and season with ½ teaspoon of salt, the coriander, and pepper. Sauté until the onions and chard stems are soft and the onions translucent, but not browned, about 5 minutes. Add the minced garlic and sauté just until fragrant, about 1 minute. Add the Swiss chard leaves and ½ cup / 2 g of the cilantro, and sauté for about 2 minutes, or just until the chard is bright green. Sprinkle in the flour and stir to combine, still over the heat.

Add the Swiss chard mixture to the lentils, stir in the lemon juice, and heat through for just a few minutes (keeping the chard leaves bright green) before turning off the heat.

Let the soup cool for about 10 minutes. Taste and adjust the seasonings, if needed. To serve, sprinkle each bowl with some of the remaining cilantro.

Toasted Bulgur with Poached Chicken and Cinnamon

This is known as chicken and *smeed*, one of those go-to dishes, especially when the pantry is low and a warm, healthy, and inviting meal is in order. Serve this dish with a romaine salad dressed with lemon and oil (page 80), labneh (page 29), and pita bread. The smeed is remarkably versatile—Aunt Louise throws in any good thing she has on hand to brighten her smeed, from frozen peas to diced koosa and chickpeas. If you don't want to use the chicken breasts that make the broth here, substitute prepared chicken or vegetable broth instead, then stir a couple of cups of shredded chicken pieces from a roasted chicken (purchased or homemade) into the cooked smeed.

Makes 6 servings

2 bone-in chicken breasts, skin on

2 teaspoons kosher salt, divided

2 tablespoons salted butter

2 cups / 380 g coarse bulgur (#3 or #4 grade)

Few grinds of black pepper

1 cinnamon stick

In a 3-quart / 3 L saucepan, cover the chicken by 1 inch / 2.5 cm with cold water and add a teaspoon of the salt. Bring to a boil over medium-high heat. Skim off any foam, and reduce the heat to medium-low with a slow-moving simmer so as not to overcook the chicken. Poach the chicken for 20 minutes, skimming as needed, until it is partially cooked through.

Remove the chicken from the liquid and reserve 4 cups / 950 mL of the broth. When the chicken has cooled enough to handle, cut or shred it into 1- to 2-inch / 2.5 to 5 cm pieces, discarding the skin and bone.

Add the butter and the bulgur to the empty saucepan, melting the butter over medium heat until it foams up and sizzles. Stir the bulgur constantly until it turns light golden brown. Take care not to take the wheat to deep golden brown, or it will taste bitter.

Add the chicken, 4 cups / 950 mL of broth, a teaspoon of salt, pepper, and the cinnamon stick. Stir, cover, and bring to a boil. Reduce the heat and simmer until all of the broth is absorbed, about 20 minutes. Taste and adjust the seasoning, if needed. Remove the cinnamon stick and serve the bulgur immediately.

Grains and Legumes

Mujadara with Crispy Onions

Make mujadara with rice or coarse bulgur; the method is the same either way, and both are delicious. There is some debate as to how far the onions should be taken in the caramelization process. They must be dark, very dark golden brown. In the end, some of the onions will verge on burnt, and others won't seem quite golden all over, which is fine. Mujadara is delicious eaten with labneh, flatbread, a crisp green salad, and if you want to get fancy, some crispy fried onions on top.

Makes 8 servings

1 cup / 200 g small brown or green lentils, sorted and rinsed

4 cups / 950 mL water, divided

¼ cup / 60 mL safflower or canola oil

2 large yellow onions, diced (4 cups / 540 g)

1 teaspoon kosher salt, plus more to taste

1 cup / 190 g coarse bulgur (#3 or #4 grade) or long-grain white rice

Few grinds of black pepper

1 tablespoon extra-virgin olive oil

For the fried onion garnish (optional):

Safflower or canola oil, for frying

1 large yellow onion cut in very thin rings

Place the lentils in a small saucepan with 2 cups / 475 mL of the water. Bring the water to a boil over high heat, and then reduce the heat and simmer, covered, until the lentils are par-cooked (al dente to the bite; they will finish cooking in a later step), 10 to 12 minutes. Remove from the heat and set the lentils in their cooking liquid aside.

In a large sauté pan with a lid, heat the oil over medium-high heat. Add the diced onions and cook until the onions are dark golden brown (darker than typical caramelized onions), about 40 minutes, stirring frequently. Sprinkle the onions with a teaspoon of salt as they cook.

Carefully pour in the remaining 2 cups / 475 mL of water. Bring the water to a boil over high heat, and then reduce the heat to low and simmer for 2 minutes.

Stir the bulgur and par-cooked lentils with their liquid into the onion mixture. Cover and bring back to a boil. Stir in a healthy pinch of salt and the black pepper. Reduce the heat to low, cover, and cook until the liquid has been absorbed and the bulgur and lentils are cooked through, about 20 minutes. The texture of the cooked bulgur and lentils will be slightly al dente. Remove from the heat and season to taste with more salt and pepper, if needed. Serve the mujadara hot, warm, or room temperature drizzled with olive oil.

For the fried onion garnish, heat the oil over medium-high heat to 375°F / 190°C in a small saucepan (the small saucepan reduces the amount of oil needed for depth). When a small piece of onion bubbles vigorously, the oil is ready. Fry the onions in batches until they are golden brown. Transfer the onions to a paper towel-lined plate, and then arrange them on top of the mujadara.

MMM MMM MMMUJADARA

I wish I could tell you a warm and fuzzy story about how mujadara (pronounced muh-JUD-da-da) has always been a special dish in the family. Truth be told, mujadara was far from my favorite growing up. Lentils didn't hold a lot of kid-appeal among my siblings; they were to be avoided. We children walked far away from the table when lentils were on it, same way I did when I'd see a dog nearby. You'd wonder where I was headed and then realize I was circling the park, walking far out of my way to avoid that dog. It might bite.

I try to remind myself of my childhood aversion to mujadara whenever a child in the family looks in terror at something placed before them on their plates. Usually we beg them to at least taste it, or offer a gentle reminder of *Green Eggs and Ham*, to which the response is something along the lines of "eggs are NOT green." It's not like we've tried too hard to feed any of them mujadara; we're just talking about, say, mashed potatoes, or green bits of anything in anything, or any scoop of one food touching another—and at least one of those kids has gone kind of crazy, as though a huge, fierce dog is going to sink his teeth in and never let go.

During my graduate school years, I was enamored of my first apartment and most of all with having a kitchen to call my own. I got into some heavy thinking about all kinds of things, and for a short time, swore off meat (religion too). Mom was concerned, mostly about my ability to maintain good nutrition, especially knowing my propensity at that point to skip meals in favor of candy or nothing at all. But her response was one that I've never forgotten. Instead of asking me in disbelief how I would survive without kibbeh, she gave me a vegetarian cookbook. This was the first

cookbook to grace my bookshelf; it was beautiful, and I was mesmerized. She also gave me the recipe for mujadara, and told me about why it's so good for you. The combination of lentils with rice or cracked wheat forms a perfect protein, along with the fiber and other nutrients much needed in any diet, especially one that doesn't include meat. Her approach to my swearing off of meat (we won't go into what she thought about me dumping my religion, which was happily short-lived) charmed me into walking right up to the lentils, as if they were a feared dog, only to discover how wonderful they could be.

My first tries at mujadara were just okay, producing a mush that tasted fine but gave off an aroma from the hot oil and deeply caramelized (or in my case, burnt) onions that was so strong it permeated the woodwork. I think I can still smell those early batches in my hair today. I've since discovered that in some areas of Lebanon, mujadara is in fact pureed, so my mush could probably have passed for something other than a mistake. But then Aunt Rita casually mentioned that she deeply caramelized her onions in vegetable oil because with the olive oil's lower smoke point, the onions, which need to get very dark, burn easily and the whole house smells of it for days. A revelation.

One of the great things about mujadara is that you can make it on a whim with ingredients you likely already have in the pantry. This is peasant food, food that developed out of need. But in the hands of the Lebanese women who throughout history have known instinctively how to make all food taste good, the ingredients were transformed into a beloved dish, one that, approached with a little gentleness and charm, could coax even the most stubborn palate into submission.

Freekeh with Tomato and Chickpeas

This dish is a Lebanese classic made with bulgur, but I find it a perfect way to cook freekeh. I found some skeptical eaters when I first started making this freekeh dish, but that was only until they had a taste; from then on they realized they can and do like to eat freekeh. Freekeh is roasted green wheat that is a bit chewier and more substantial in texture than bulgur. It is super healthful, high in fiber and protein, and cooks up just like rice and bulgur. Serve this as you would rice as a side dish, or as a main dish with a salad.

Makes 4 servings

¼ cup / 65 g tomato paste

¼ cup / 60 mL warm water

2 tablespoons extra-virgin olive oil

1 medium-size yellow onion, finely chopped

½ teaspoon kosher salt

¼ teaspoon ground cinnamon

1 cup / 200 g freekeh (cracked roasted green wheat)

2 cups / 475 mL chicken stock, vegetable stock, or water

1 cup / 150 g chickpeas (canned or cooked from dried soaked chickpeas), skinned (page 43)

1 cinnamon stick

In a small bowl, whisk the tomato paste with ¼ cup / 60 mL warm water.

In a 2-quart / 2 L saucepan, heat the oil over medium heat. Add the onion and salt, and cook until the onion is soft and translucent, but not browned at all. Stir in the ground cinnamon.

Add the freekeh and stir, coating it with the juices of the onion mixture. Stir in the tomato paste mixture. Add the stock or water and the chickpeas and cinnamon stick, stirring to combine everything. Cover the pot with a lid and bring the liquid to a boil.

Reduce the heat to low and simmer until the freekeh is tender, cooked through, and has absorbed all of the liquid, about 25 minutes. Remove from the heat and let it stand, covered, for about 10 minutes before serving.

Fresh Herb Falafel with Tahini-Yogurt Sauce

What a fantastic discovery homemade falafel is! Completely fresh and such a difference from falafel in restaurants, because of the copious fresh herbs and balance of spices. We've never cooked with cumin in my extended Lebanese family, but here you can add a pinch if you like. The dried, shelled fava beans needed for homemade falafel are the large skinless white variety (page 243). If you have trouble finding these, simply double the amount of chickpeas and leave the fava beans out. Begin making the falafel a day in advance to give the dry chickpeas and beans a good soak. You can make the tahini sauce up to three days in advance. An ice cream scoop works great as an alternative to the traditional falafel scoop. Be careful not to make the falafel too large, or they won't cook through to the center. They're delicious tucked into your own pita (page 192) with pink pickled turnips (page 206) and a drizzle of Tahini-Yogurt Sauce (page 34).

Makes 10 falafel

½ cup / 100 g dry chickpeas

½ cup / 100 g dry shelled fava beans

1 teaspoon kosher salt

Big handful of fresh mint leaves (about 20 leaves)

1 bunch fresh flat-leaf parsley leaves

½ bunch fresh cilantro leaves

1 small jalapeño, ribs and seeds removed and coarsely chopped, or ½ teaspoon cayenne pepper

1 garlic clove, minced

1 small yellow onion, coarsely chopped

1 tablespoon sesame seeds

1 teaspoon baking soda

3 cups / 700 mL safflower or canola oil, for frying

1 recipe Tahini-Yogurt Sauce (page 34)

In a medium bowl, cover the chickpeas and fava beans with cool water by 3 inches / 7.5 cm. Soak them overnight and up to 24 hours.

Thoroughly drain the chickpeas and fava beans. In the food processor, process them with a teaspoon of salt until they are ground to a coarse crumb. Add the mint, parsley, cilantro, jalapeño, garlic, onion, and sesame seeds and pulse until the mixture is finely ground to a moist crumb. Transfer the mixture to a bowl, stir in the baking soda, and chill for at least 30 minutes or up to 1 day.

Heat the oil to 375°F / 190°C in a 3-quart / 3 L saucepan or sauté pan until a dropped pinch of herb bubbles dramatically. Using an ice cream scoop or a large spoon, pack the falafel mixture tightly into the scoop to form 2-inch / 5 cm ovals, and fry a few at a time until they are golden brown, flipping them over with tongs as soon as they are browned on one side. Remove the falafel from the oil with the tongs to a paper towel-lined plate, and fry the remaining falafel.

Serve the falafel hot with the tahini sauce on the side.

Fava Beans and Chickpeas with Garlic, Lemon, and Olive Oil

This dish, known as *foul medammes* (pronounced FOOL meh-DAHM-mess), is a ubiquitous breakfast or brunch dish throughout the Middle East. It's an unusual approach to breakfast for most of us, but it's so flavorful and packed with nutrients, fiber, and protein that it might just be your new go-to jumpstart for delicious energy to start the day. We typically eat it smeared on pita bread. Of course, the beans are good and good for you, any time of the day.

Makes 6 servings

2 cups / 300 g cooked chickpeas, skinned (page 43), divided

1 large garlic clove, minced, divided

¼ teaspoon kosher salt, divided

Juice of 1 lemon

2 cups / 300 g cooked fava beans (cooking liquid reserved)

2 tablespoons extra-virgin olive oil

2 tablespoons finely chopped fresh flat-leaf parsley

1 small sweet onion, half of it finely diced and half sliced

4 radishes, thinly sliced, divided

½ cup / 75 g kalamata olives, for serving

In a small mixing bowl, coarsely mash half of the chickpeas with half of the garlic, ⅛ teaspoon of salt, and the lemon juice using a potato masher, fork, or pestle. Spoon this mixture into a serving bowl.

If you're using canned fava beans, drain half of the liquid and pour the rest with the favas into a small saucepan. If you're using fava beans that you've cooked, add ½ cup / 120 mL of the cooking liquid to the pan. Heat the fava beans with the rest of the garlic over medium heat, mashing about half of the mixture to make a thick porridge with lots of whole beans still remaining. Stir in the remaining whole chickpeas and ⅛ teaspoon salt, and heat through, stirring constantly.

Pour the fava bean mixture over the chickpea mash in the serving bowl, and pour the olive oil evenly over the top. Arrange the parsley, chopped onion, and half of the radishes on top of the beans decoratively.

Serve the beans immediately with a small plate of sliced sweet onion, the remaining radishes, and the olives.

Crunchy Roasted Za'atar Chickpeas

This is healthy snack food at its very best. Chickpeas are packed with fiber, protein, and vitamins, and they are addictively good with za'atar—knocking other coated crunchy snacks out of the ballpark in both nutrition and taste.

Makes 4 servings

2 cups / 300 g cooked chickpeas

1 tablespoon extra-virgin olive oil

2 tablespoons za'atar

½ teaspoon kosher salt

Rinse the chickpeas and spread them out on a paper towel to dry out for an hour or so, patting them dry with another paper towel as well.

Heat the oven to 400°F / 200°C. Line a heavy rimmed sheet pan with parchment paper and spread out the chickpeas evenly on the pan. Bake them in the center of the oven for about 30 minutes, stirring and rotating every 10 minutes. Taste a chickpea or two. If they are crunchy, they're done. If not, keep going. The chickpeas will continue to get crunchy as they cool, too.

Place the hot chickpeas in a bowl and drizzle with olive oil, za'atar, and salt. Store any cooled leftovers in an airtight container for up to a week.

Lebanese Vermicelli Rice

While this cinnamon-scented rice is always made to accompany dishes like Eggplant with Lamb, Tomato, and Pine Nuts (page 98) and Green Bean and Lamb Stew (page 117), it is also a delicate, comforting dish alongside grilled or roasted meats and vegetables. Basmati rice also works well here; just be sure to rinse the rice numerous times before cooking it to remove a good bit of the starch, or it will turn out gummy.

Makes 6 to 8 servings

1 cup / 190 g long-grain rice

1 tablespoon salted butter

¼ cup / 35 g broken dry vermicelli noodles (2-inch / 5 cm pieces)

½ teaspoon kosher salt

2 cups / 475 mL chicken stock or water

1 cinnamon stick

Melt the butter with the dry vermicelli in a 2-quart / 2 L saucepan over medium-high heat, stirring constantly until the butter is nutty-brown and the vermicelli turns golden.

Stir in the rice, coating it with the butter. Add the salt, broth, and cinnamon stick. Bring the mixture to a boil, reduce the heat and simmer, covered, for about 20 minutes, or until all of the liquid is absorbed and the rice is cooked through. Remove the cinnamon stick and serve the rice hot.

Grains and Legumes

Pastry & Sweets

Rose Water Meringues
with Roasted Rhubarb

Sticky Date Cake with
Warm Orange Blossom–Caramel Sauce

Walnut Baklawa Diamonds

Rice Pudding with Dried Cherries
and Pistachios

Crunchy Sesame Cookies

Pomegranate Rose Sorbet

Graybeh (Shortbread Cookies)

Ma'moul (Molded Date Cookies)

Salted Pistachio Bark
with Dried Apricots

Knafeh with Melted Cheese
and Orange Blossom Syrup

Mandarin Orange Frozen Yogurt

Nougat Glacé with Sweet Cherries
and Candied Almonds

Spiced Sweet Bread with
Rose Water Milk Glaze

Sugared Anise Donuts

Labneh with Orange, Avocado,
Pomegranate, and Honey

Labneh with Tart Cherry–Rose
Water Compote

Stone Fruit with Flower Waters
and Shaved Coconut

Rose Water Meringues with Roasted Rhubarb

This beautiful dessert is a heaven of texture, flavor, and color—worthy of gracing any special gathering of people you love. The sweet clouds of meringue are balanced perfectly with tart roasted rhubarb; a subtle infusion of rose water enhances the flavor of both. It's easiest to separate the eggs while they are cold to ensure no traces of yolk remain in the whites, and then bring the whites to room temperature. This can be done swiftly in the microwave for 5 seconds, if need be. The meringues can be made several hours or a day in advance and kept in an airtight container. They also freeze well for up to 3 months. Serve them cold from the freezer, or thawed at room temperature for 30 minutes.

Makes 6 servings

For the rose water meringues:

- 2 egg whites, at room temperature
- ¼ teaspoon cream of tartar
- Pinch of kosher salt
- 3 drops rose water
- ¾ cup / 150 g granulated sugar

For the roasted rhubarb:

- 1½ pounds / 675 g rhubarb, cut into 1-inch / 2.5 cm pieces (about 4 cups)
- ¾ cup / 150 g granulated sugar
- Grated zest of 1 organic lemon
- ½ teaspoon rose water

For the whipped cream:

- 1 cup / 240 mL heavy whipping cream, chilled
- 1 teaspoon granulated sugar
- 2 tablespoons finely chopped roasted, salted pistachios, for garnish

Arrange a rack in the center of the oven and preheat the oven to 200°F / 95°C. Line two rimmed sheet pans with parchment paper.

In the clean, dry mixing bowl of an electric mixer fitted with the whisk attachment, or with a handheld mixer, whisk the egg whites, cream of tartar, and salt on low speed until they are foamy, about 3 minutes. Add the rose water, and then increase the speed to medium and continue beating until the egg whites are bright white and hold a soft peak, about 3 more minutes. Add the sugar slowly, one tablespoon at a time, with the mixer on high speed. Beat the egg whites until they are glossy and hold a stiff peak, another 3 minutes.

Using a large, clean spoon, scoop six dollops of meringue, about ½ cup / 120 mL each, onto one of the prepared sheet pans 3 inches / 7.5 cm apart. Use the back of a clean teaspoon to shape and create a well in the center of each meringue, like a bird's nest.

Bake the meringues for 60 minutes, or until they are dry. Turn off the oven and prop it open with a wooden spoon to let the meringues continue to dry for 30 minutes longer.

To roast the rhubarb, heat the oven to 400°F / 200°C. Meanwhile, in a large mixing bowl, coat the rhubarb thoroughly with the sugar, lemon zest, and rose water and set it aside to macerate for 10 minutes.

Spread the macerated rhubarb evenly on the second prepared sheet pan. Roast it for 20 minutes, or until it is bright pink and tender but still holds its shape. Remove the rhubarb from the oven and let it cool for a few minutes, or up to an hour. Any longer resting time, and the juices from the rhubarb may become too thick to spoon over the meringues.

While the rhubarb roasts, whip the cream in a medium bowl with the sugar until soft peaks form. Chill the whipped cream until you're ready to serve the meringues (the whipped cream can be made several hours in advance and chilled; if it melts some, use a whisk to whip it a bit again).

To serve the meringues, place each meringue on a dessert plate. Place a dollop of whipped cream in the well of the meringues. Divide the rhubarb evenly among the meringues, spooning the rhubarb over the whipped cream. Drizzle the rhubarb juice decoratively over the edges of the meringues and onto the plate. Sprinkle pistachios over each meringue and serve immediately.

Photos on following pages: Rose Water Meringues with Roasted Rhubarb (left) and Graybeh (page 164) and Ma'moul (page 166) Cookies (right).

Pastry and Sweets

Sticky Date Cake with Warm Orange Blossom–Caramel Sauce

Remember the poke-and-pour cakes of another era, using colorful gelatin and white cake? We're poking and pouring here too, but with a brown sugar caramel that echoes the flavors of the moist date cake. Even the wariest of date-eaters will spoon this cake up with abandon. When I brought big slices to lunch with some of my oldest childhood friends, they unanimously declared dates on their don't-eat-those list. But then they took a bite, and ended up eating the entire cake before lunch.

Makes 8 servings

For the cake:

¼ cup / 60 g unsalted butter, at room temperature, plus 1 tablespoon to coat the pan

1¼ cups / 300 mL water

1¾ cups / 260 g chopped pitted dates (about 20 Medjool dates)

1 teaspoon baking soda

1 cup / 130 g unbleached all-purpose flour

1 teaspoon baking powder

¼ teaspoon kosher salt

½ packed cup / 110 g light brown sugar

2 large eggs

½ teaspoon vanilla extract

For the caramel sauce:

6 tablespoons / 90 g unsalted butter

⅛ teaspoon kosher salt

1 cup / 240 mL heavy whipping cream

¾ packed cup / 115 g light brown sugar

Few drops orange blossom water

For the whipped cream:

1 cup / 240 mL heavy whipping cream

1 tablespoon granulated sugar

Arrange a rack in the center of the oven and preheat the oven to 350°F / 175°C. Coat an 8-inch / 20 cm cake pan with about ½ tablespoon of the butter. Line the bottom with parchment, and then lightly butter the top of the parchment with the remaining ½ tablespoon of butter.

Heat the water in a medium saucepan over high heat to boiling. Add the dates, bring the mixture back to a boil, and then reduce the heat to medium and simmer for 5 minutes to soften the dates, giving them a stir every so often. Remove the dates from the heat and stir in the baking soda (the mixture will foam up a little). Set this aside.

In a small bowl, whisk the flour, baking powder, and salt.

In the bowl of an electric mixer, beat the ¼ cup butter and the brown sugar on high speed until the mixture is light and fluffy, about 2 minutes, stopping to scrape down the sides of the bowl mid-way through beating. Add the eggs one at a time, mixing thoroughly after each addition and stopping to scrape the bowl as you go; the mixture may look slightly curdled, but it's fine.

Add the dates and vanilla and continue to beat, scraping down the bowl. Slowly add the flour to the mixture on low speed, and thoroughly combine. The batter will be somewhat thin.

Pour the batter into the prepared pan and bake for 30 to 40 minutes, or until the cake is golden brown and springs back when touched in the center.

While the cake bakes, make the caramel sauce. In a small saucepan, melt the butter over medium heat. Add the salt, cream, brown sugar, and orange blossom water and bring it to a boil, and then reduce the heat to a simmer, whisking constantly until the mixture is combined and slightly thickened, about 5 minutes. Reserve about ½ cup / 120 mL of the caramel sauce for serving.

While the cake is still warm, poke it liberally all over with a toothpick or skewer, all the way out to the edges. Spoon a few tablespoons of the caramel sauce evenly over the surface of the cake all the way out to the edges, one tablespoon at a time and using the back of the spoon to spread the caramel around while it is absorbed by the cake. Let the cake rest for 15 minutes.

Turn the cake out onto a platter, with the bottom side facing up, and poke this side liberally with a toothpick or skewer, again all the way out to the edges, and slowly spoon several tablespoons of the caramel sauce over the cake in the same way you did on the other side, one tablespoon at a time to let the caramel absorb into the cake. Let some of the caramel drip decoratively down the sides of the cake. Allow the cake to rest for 15 minutes or up to several hours, uncovered, before serving.

Make the whipped cream by beating the cream with the sugar in a medium bowl until soft peaks form. Chill the whipped cream until you are ready to serve the cake.

Reheat the reserved caramel sauce before serving if it has thickened too much to pour. Cut the cake into wedges and serve each piece with a spoonful of caramel sauce and whipped cream on top.

Walnut Baklawa Diamonds

Baklawa is the ultimate Lebanese pastry, on the table for all holidays and special occasions. The clarified butter, orange blossom syrup, and nuts can be prepared well in advance and kept refrigerated or frozen; this makes assembling the baklawa a much quicker process. The method here—my Aunt Rita's way—is remarkably simple and works wonderfully. She did not butter every layer as is traditional, but rather poured the butter over the assembled and cut pastry before baking. Rita baked and sold her trays of baklawa throughout Lansing, Michigan, and to listen to her describe her herculean efforts was mind-blowing: every December, she clarified fifty pounds of butter—fifty!—to remove the milk solids that burn in baklawa. Necessity inspired her to simplify the baklawa-assembly process, and the results were so delectable that she was renowned for baking the finest pastry you could eat without ever having buttered each layer. For that I consider her one of the greatest innovators of our era!

Makes about 40 pieces

- 1 pound / 500 g frozen phyllo dough (such as Athens), in 9 x 14-inch / 23 x 35 cm sheets
- 3 cups / 450 g , lightly toasted
- ½ cup / 100 g granulated sugar
- ¾ cup / 180 g clarified butter (page 41), melted, divided
- 1 recipe orange blossom syrup (page 40), chilled

To thaw the frozen phyllo, refrigerate it overnight, and then bring it to room temperature for an hour before using it. Don't open the wrapped packages of phyllo until just before you are ready to assemble the baklawa.

Chop the nuts coarsely in the food processor with a few pulses, taking care not to pulverize them to a powder. Some nut-dust is unavoidable, but it is better to have a few nuts that need to be broken by hand than to process too much.

In a medium bowl, combine the walnuts and sugar, stirring until all of the nuts are coated.

Move an oven rack to the middle position and preheat the oven to 350°F / 175°C.

To assemble the baklawa, cut open one sleeve of the phyllo and carefully unroll it on top of its plastic wrapping.

Using kitchen shears, trim the phyllo along the short side by 1 inch / 2.5 cm.

Brush the bottom of a 13 x 9 x 2-inch / 33 x 23 x 5 cm metal pan with a tablespoon of the clarified butter. Lay the stack of trimmed phyllo into the pan. Spread the sugared nuts over the phyllo in one even layer.

Open the second sleeve of phyllo and trim it as you did the first sleeve, by 1 inch / 2.5 cm along the short side. Lay all but 4 leaves of this phyllo over the nuts, and cover the remaining 4 leaves of phyllo with a very lightly dampened paper towel or kitchen towel.

Brush the top of the phyllo in the pan with about a tablespoon of clarified butter, coating the sheet of phyllo completely. Lay one of the remaining sheets of phyllo on top and brush that layer with another tablespoon of butter. Repeat this for the remaining 3 phyllo leaves.

Using the tip of a sharp serrated knife, slice the baklawa into diamonds. To do this, lightly score the top of the phyllo with cut marks before actually cutting, to guide you. On the short end of the pan, mark off six rows with 5 score marks the length of the pan, dividing it first in half, and then each half into 3 rows for a total of six. Do the same thing diagonally crosswise on the long side of the pan, scoring about 12 diagonal rows, which form the diamonds. Use your dominant hand to cut and the other hand to hold the phyllo down on either side of the blade while cutting. Be sure to cut all the way through to the bottom of the pan, so that the butter will seep through all layers. Hold the knife nearly perpendicular to the pastry, cutting down with the tip into the phyllo and nuts.

Pour the remaining melted clarified butter evenly over the baklawa. Allow the butter to settle in for a minute or two. Bake the baklawa until it is deep golden brown and the phyllo deep in the diamond cuts is no longer bright white, about 50 minutes, rotating the baklawa halfway through baking.

Remove the pan from the oven and immediately pour the cold orange blossom syrup evenly over the baklawa. When the pastry is just cool enough to handle, cut away a few of the uneven edge morsels to eat warm (the baker's reward . . . this delicious, buttery moment alone makes the whole process worth it). Let the baklawa cool, uncovered, for several hours.

Cut the pieces of baklawa from the pan as needed, using a sharp chef's knife to cut out the diamonds. The diamonds look lovely arranged in a circle, with their points facing the center, on a platter. Keep the baklawa lightly, not tightly, covered in the pan with plastic wrap or topped loosely with a layer of waxed paper for up to 2 weeks.

Rice Pudding with Dried Cherries and Pistachios

Rice pudding is synonymous with my mother, who considers it one of life's great comforts. When you taste a spoonful, warm, right from the pan, you'll see why. Goes down easy. And you don't have to make it as rich as my mother does; the pudding can be made leaner by substituting lower fat milk, or even skim milk, for the whole milk and cream. Crunchy Sesame Cookies (page 161) are a nice accompaniment to the pudding.

Makes 8 servings

- 4½ cups / 1.1 L whole milk
- ½ cup / 120 mL heavy whipping cream
- ⅓ cup / 65 g medium-grain white rice
- 3 large eggs, lightly beaten
- 3 tablespoons cornstarch
- ¼ teaspoon kosher salt

- ½ cup / 100 g granulated sugar
- ½ teaspoon orange blossom water or vanilla extract
- ½ cup / 75 g dried tart cherries, coarsely chopped, divided
- 2 tablespoons shelled roasted, salted pistachios, finely chopped, for serving

In a 3-quart / 3 L saucepan, heat the milk and cream over medium heat just to boiling. Stir in the rice, reduce the heat, and simmer for 30 minutes uncovered, stirring occasionally.

In a small bowl, whisk the eggs, cornstarch, salt, and sugar until smooth. Temper the egg mixture by slowly stirring in ¼ cup / 60 mL of the hot rice milk. Whisk the rice mixture while you slowly pour in the tempered egg mixture, and then simmer, stirring constantly, until the pudding is slightly thickened. Stir in the orange blossom water and all but a couple of tablespoons of the dried cherries.

Serve the pudding warm, in small individual bowls topped with the chopped pistachios and reserved dried cherries, or serve the pudding chilled. To chill it, place waxed paper or plastic wrap directly against the surface of the warm pudding to prevent formation of a skin on top.

Crunchy Sesame Cookies

These biscuit-like cookies are addictive because of their crunchy texture and nutty sesame flavor. They're perfect with most any coffee or tea (pages 224 to 229). Keep the cookies crunchy by storing them, immediately after cooling, in an airtight container. They'll last several weeks that way. The dough is best used immediately after it's made.

Makes 2 dozen cookies

2¼ cups / 300 g unbleached all-purpose flour

1 teaspoon cream of tartar

1 teaspoon baking soda

¼ teaspoon kosher salt

½ cup / 120 g unsalted butter, at room temperature

⅔ cup / 135 g granulated sugar

1 large egg, at room temperature

1 teaspoon vanilla extract

1 to 2 tablespoons whole milk, lukewarm

1 cup toasted sesame seeds (page 32)

Place an oven rack in the center of the oven, and preheat the oven to 375°F / 190°C. Line two rimmed sheet pans with parchment paper.

In a small bowl, whisk the flour, cream of tartar, baking soda, and salt.

Using an electric mixer, beat the butter with the sugar on high speed until it is light and fluffy, about 2 minutes. Add the egg and vanilla and beat on medium speed another 2 minutes, or until combined, stopping to scrape down the sides of the bowl. Reduce the speed to low and add the flour mixture just until combined, and then increase the speed to medium and beat just until the mixture comes together, less than a minute. The dough will be very dry and still showing flour. Add 1 tablespoon of the milk and beat on low speed until a soft dough forms, less than a minute. Test the dough by squeezing a small ball in your hand; if it is dry and cracking, add one more tablespoon of milk and beat for less than a minute.

Place the sesame seeds in a small bowl. Shape a tablespoon of dough into a ball and flatten it, with your fingers or the bottom of a cup, to a ¼-inch- / .5 cm thick disk on an unfloured work surface. Press the disk into the sesame seeds, turning it over and onto its sides to coat it completely with sesame seeds. Repeat with the rest of the dough and sesame seeds, placing the cookies about an inch apart on the prepared pans.

Bake the first pan as soon as it is ready, continuing to make the second pan of cookies while the first one bakes.

Bake the cookies for 14 to 16 minutes, or until golden brown, rotating the pan halfway through baking. Remove the pan from the oven and cool the cookies completely on racks; they will firm up and get crunchy once they are cool. Store the cookies, immediately after they are cooled, in an airtight container for up to 1 week; they also freeze nicely in an airtight container for several months.

Pastry and Sweets

Pomegranate Rose Sorbet

Sorbets have become one of my favorite desserts in the summer; they are light, often sweet-tart, and refreshing. Pomegranate juice, enhanced to great effect with a drop of rose water, keeps this sorbet perfectly tart and not too sweet. And the color? Bright, vivid, gorgeous. It's a total pleasure serving this sorbet in little bowls to guests for dessert (and particularly beautiful topped with chopped pistachios, our favorite pink and green combination), as a palate cleanser between courses, or scooped into a celebratory punch bowl.

Makes 8 servings

¾ cup / 150 g granulated sugar

¾ cup / 180 mL warm water

¼ cup / 60 mL light corn syrup

1½ cups / 360 mL 100 percent pure pomegranate juice

Juice of 1 lemon

3 drops rose water

In a 2-quart / 2 L saucepan over medium heat, heat the sugar with the warm water until the water boils and the sugar melts. Add the corn syrup, pomegranate juice, lemon juice, and rose water and simmer for 3 minutes.

Pour the mixture into a heatproof bowl, cool for 10 minutes, and then cover and chill it until it is completely cold. Or, pour the slightly cooled mixture into a heavy-duty plastic freezer bag and immerse it in a bowl of ice water until it is completely cold.

Churn the pomegranate mixture in an ice cream maker according to the manufacturer's instructions. Chill the sorbet in the freezer in an airtight container for at least 12 hours and up to several weeks.

Graybeh (Shortbread Cookies)

The clarified butter is essential to the melt-in-your-mouth texture of this classic Lebanese cookie, so resist any urge to use regular butter. See the way to clarify butter on page 41. Graybeh can be flavored several wonderful ways, with a few drops of rose water, a combination of rose and orange blossom, or with 2 teaspoons of dried ground lavender (my favorite, and so delicate combined with the orange blossom water). Try an anise flavor with a ½ teaspoon of anise extract or ground anise seed. Of course, a teaspoon of vanilla is also delicious.

Makes about 3 dozen cookies

¾ cup / 180 g clarified butter, at room temperature (page 41)

1¼ cups / 125 g confectioners' sugar, divided

½ teaspoon kosher salt

1 teaspoon orange blossom water

1¾ cups / 228 g plus up to 3 tablespoons unbleached all-purpose flour

Place a rack in the center of the oven and preheat the oven to 325°F / 160°C. Line two heavy sheet pans (not dark metal) with parchment paper.

In an electric mixer beat the butter on high speed until it is very light and fluffy, like a lovely whipped cream, about 6 minutes. Add ¾ cup / 75 g of the confectioners' sugar and the salt and beat on high speed until the mixture is light and fluffy again, another 2 minutes. Turn the mixer off and scrape down the sides of the bowl.

With the mixer on low speed, add the orange blossom water or any flavoring you'd like to use. Add the flour ½ cup / 65 g at a time, watching for the dough to become crumbly and a bit dry, but still to hold together when squeezed. Add the additional flour if needed. If the dough is too soft, it will not hold its shape well when baked, so better to err on the side of drier, somewhat crumbly dough.

Working with the dough immediately (do not chill it, as counterintuitive as that may seem when working with butter dough), shape a quarter of the dough at a time into a compact, very narrow, flat-topped log about an inch wide and an inch tall; the dough, because of its dryness, needs to be pressed, inch by inch, into the log shape rather than rolled. It's helpful to keep one hand pressing down on the log as you press the dough into the log with the other. Cut the log with a sharp knife on the diagonal to make 1- to 2-inch / 2.5 to 5 cm diamonds. The diamonds are rather small—about an inch tall and wide, and about 2 inches long—and need to be this size in order to bake properly.

Use a spatula to transfer the diamonds to one of the prepared sheet pans and space them about 2 inches / 5 cm apart. Bake for 15 to 20 minutes, rotating the pan front to back halfway through, until the cookies are very pale golden brown. Fill the second sheet pan with the diamonds and bake those when the first batch is done.

Sift half of the remaining ½ cup / 50 g confectioners' sugar over the cookies while they are still warm, and then again once they've cooled. Or, leave the cookies bare without confectioners' sugar; they're just as delicious. Store the cookies in an airtight container for up to 1 week.

Ma'moul (Molded Date Cookies)

Coming from a long line of intense, stress-inclined Abood personalities, it doesn't surprise me that my Aunt Hilda loved to make *ma'moul*, the extraordinary molded shortbread cookies of Lebanon. She never considered herself a baker, but come Christmas and Easter, she got after it big time. The molded ma'moul cookie was a favorite (it can be made with this date filling, or with the nuts used for baklawa, page 158), and once I got into the process of banging out my own, I could understand why. Perhaps the most crucial aspect of making ma'moul—releasing the cookies from the molds—was a stress-relieving attraction for her, as it is for me: Dust the mold (see page 242 for sources) with flour, fill it with a date-stuffed ball of baby-soft dough to make the impression, and then slam the mold face-down against the (sturdy) table two or three times, until the cookie comes out. Whew. I feel better already.

Makes about 36 cookies

1 tablespoon unsalted butter

¼ cup / 60 mL water

2 cups / 300 g Medjool dates, pitted and chopped

1 cup / 240 g clarified butter, at room temperature (page 41)

1 teaspoon orange blossom water or vanilla extract

6 tablespoons granulated sugar, divided

2 cups / 260 g unbleached all-purpose flour, sifted, plus more as needed

1 tablespoon milk

1 cup / 100 g confectioners' sugar

In a small saucepan, bring the unsalted butter and water to a boil over medium-high heat. Stir in the dates, reduce the heat to low, and simmer until the dates are softened, about 2 minutes. Cool to room temperature, or chill them in an airtight container for up to 2 days.

Using an electric mixer, beat the clarified butter on medium-high speed until it is light and fluffy like whipped cream, about 6 minutes (that's not a typo! A long whip is called for). Enjoy the beauty. Add the orange blossom water and 3 tablespoons of the granulated sugar and beat for another 2 minutes.

Now working with a wooden spoon rather than the mixer, sift in the flour and gently stir it into the butter. Add the milk, and then add more flour by the tablespoon until the dough is pliable, kneading it for another minute or two. You should be able to make a ball of dough that will flatten in your floured palm without melting into your hand (if it's too soft, add a tablespoon of flour) or without cracking (if it's too dry, add up to a table-spoon of milk). Chill the dough, covered in a bowl or wrapped in plastic, for 30 minutes.

Place a rack in the middle position in the oven and preheat the oven to 325°F / 165°C. Line two heavy sheet pans (not dark metal) with parchment.

To form the ma'moul, pinch off about a table-spoon / 15 g, walnut-sized piece of the chilled dough. Flour the palms of your hands to prevent the dough from sticking, and flatten the dough in your palm to make a small (about 2-inch / 5 cm) disk. Place about a teaspoon of the date filling in the center of the dough, and then enclose the filling in the dough, stretching the dough a little to seal it evenly around the filling, making a half-moon shape.

Flour the ma'moul mold generously so that all grooves are coated. Gently nestle the smooth, stuffed-side of the dough into the mold cavity, with the seam-side facing up. Using a light touch, press the dough into the mold—it doesn't take much pressure for the dough to take the form of the mold. Flatten the exposed dough and wipe away any excess dough with your fingers, making sure that the edge of the mold cavity is clear of dough, for a defined cookie edge. You will get a feel for how much dough your mold takes, and how much filling you need, as you make a few of the cookies.

Turn the mold over and slam it against the work surface until the cookie falls out. Repeat this process with the remaining dough and cookies, transferring the cookies to the sheet pans with a spatula.

Bake one sheet pan of cookies at a time, until they are pale in color with just a hint of golden brown on the bottoms. Check the bottoms by lifting one with a flat metal spatula after 10 min-utes, and then again every minute or so for another 3 to 4 minutes, depending on the size of your cookies.

Sift confectioners' sugar over the cookies lightly while they are still warm, and then again when they are room temperature. Store them in an airtight container, where they will stay nice for at least 1 week.

GEO. ABOWD & SONS, CONFECTIONERS

The last time my Uncle Tom saw his father before he died, he was at the stove. Grandpa (my Jiddo who did not want to be called the Arabic *Jiddo*, but rather the all-American "Grandpa") was in his mid-80s, and he had something important to tell his physician son, so he sent for him at the hospital. Tom rushed off the job, a little miffed at what could be so important.

When he arrived, Grandpa was working quietly at the stove, melting chocolate. "I wanted to be sure you know how this is done," he told Tom, and proceeded to demonstrate the proper technique to temper chocolate for dipping.

My grandfather, Richard George Abowd, became a confectioner as a teenage boy. I imagine he wasn't much older than my nephew at twelve, his great-grandson and namesake. I use the old-school word "confectioner" whenever I can, and I take pride in telling people: "My grandfather was a confectioner." Such a description lends a kind of stamp of approval to my own pursuits, and a heritage that speaks to authenticity.

Confections were not, however, my grandfather's idea of his destiny. He wanted to study, and he wanted to study law, at the University of Michigan. From the time he came to Michigan's Upper Peninsula in 1896, a five-year-old on the arm of his mother (Afifa, herself just a teen girl, but a strong one, a tough one), he started preparing. He learned to read, write, and speak English in an Arabic-only household. He worked jobs to save money so that he could make his way to Minnesota, where he would start the high school college-prep program at St. Thomas Academy. Things were looking bright until the day, not long after he arrived, when he was called to the headmaster's office. Young Richard's parents were there, and they would be leaving immediately with their son.

They were in search of a business opportunity and a better economy, and their destination was Fostoria, Ohio, where a Lebanese friend was going to help my grandfather open a candy store. Richard had the smarts and the language to make a better go of things than his parents had on the cold, harsh, rather untillable land they had tried to farm in the U.P.

The shop window was emblazoned not with my grandfather's young name, but rather his father's name. My great-grandfather George would sit in his chair by the cash register and give the chocolates away to the little children who came in,

much to Richard's irritation after all of the work he put into making them, no doubt swiftly, for a profit.

A Hershey chocolate salesman taught Grandpa to temper the chocolate, and about the sorts of inclusions (nuts, marshmallows, dried fruit) that taste good chocolate-covered. When he married my grandmother Alice, Grandpa showed her how to temper chocolate, and she was known to dip everything in sight in chocolate. It was a family affair. The children would help and carry the sheet pans of wet candies to the back stairs to cool and dry, just as I did as a child when my mother dipped chocolates.

I remember my grandmother's pretzels, coated in white chocolate and resting on waxed paper to dry in the basement of their home on Maple Street. That was quite possibly my first taste of salty-sweet pleasure. I was five years old. My mom and Uncle Tom said they never saw their mother eat a bite of the candy, not one bite. She made it and made it and made some more, but the candy was boxed and given away or eaten by the family. The joy was in the doing.

Once his candy shop became nicely established, Grandpa was "strongly encouraged" to hand the business off to his brother, who proceeded to run it into the ground while Grandpa moved on to something else that would support his own family (a hotel, The New Ohio Hotel).

The University of Michigan became relegated to my grandfather's unrequited dreams, one of those lifelong unmet ambitions that can drive a man to bitterness, or at least to drink. Instead, Richard gave his own seven children the university education he had wanted so badly for himself. They went on to give their own children—many, many of them (I am one of 70 first cousins)—extraordinary educations that their father would be proud of. Meanwhile my grandfather was a self-educated man, reading several newspapers every day sitting at his desk at the hotel, and engaging in discussions about all manner of subjects with everyone who would talk, especially his loyal weekly Rotarians.

Yet just before he died, Grandpa had something important on his mind. His thoughts no doubt ran to so many of his life events, and what could have, should have, would have happened, if only . . . . But his mind also went to what *did* happen, the perfected techniques of dipping chocolates, a confectioner's culinary heritage worth passing on.

Salted Pistachio Bark with Dried Apricots

It's been great fun passing on chocolate-making techniques in the family, especially with my brother Dick (my grandfather's namesake) and his wife and family. They are chocolate aficionados, dipping summer berries and enjoying chocolate-tastings at the kitchen counter on a whim. Even at their young ages, the children appreciate a good dark chocolate sprinkled with salt. To temper the chocolate, you'll need an instant-read thermometer. If your chocolate is tempered properly, the bark will have a nice sheen and will break apart with a snap. If not, the bark may seem fudgy and not quite dry, but it's still delicious. In that case, chill the bark and break it apart once it's cold, and then store it in the refrigerator.

Makes about 4 dozen pieces

- 24 ounces / 680 g high-quality dark chocolate (at least 58 percent cacao), finely chopped, divided
- ½ cup / 75 g shelled roasted, salted pistachios, coarsely chopped, divided
- ½ cup / 75 g finely chopped dried apricots, divided
- Sea salt (such as Maldon), for finishing

Line a sheet pan with a Silpat or parchment paper.

In a double boiler or a mixing bowl set snugly over a saucepan, heat a couple of inches of water (without letting the water touch the bottom of the bowl) in the lower saucepan to boiling. Turn off the heat, and place the bowl of the double boiler on top of the saucepan.

Place two-thirds of the chocolate in the top of the double boiler and melt it, stirring occasionally, from the steam heat of the boiled water beneath. Heat the chocolate to 110°F / 43°C, using an instant-read thermometer.

Remove the bowl from the saucepan, wiping the water from the bottom of the bowl. Stir in the remaining chopped chocolate, a handful at a time, stirring occasionally until the chocolate is cooled to 84°F / 29°C. The cooling process can take up to 30 minutes.

Reheat the water in the saucepan until it steams and is just below the boil, and then remove the pan from the heat and replace the bowl on top of the saucepan. Heat the chocolate back up just slightly, to 94°F / 34°C, which happens quickly. Working quickly, stir in half of the chopped pistachios and apricots, and then pour the chocolate mixture onto the prepared pan, scraping the bowl and spreading the chocolate out to ¼-inch / .5 cm thickness.

Immediately, so that the nuts and dried fruit will stick, scatter all the remaining chopped pistachios (and their dust) and dried apricots evenly over the chocolate. Sprinkle the sea salt evenly over the top. Gently press down on the nuts, fruit, and salt to secure them in the bark. Cool the bark completely, and then break it into pieces. Store the bark in an airtight container for several months.

Knafeh with Melted Cheese and Orange Blossom Syrup

There are several different ways *knafeh* with cheese is made (just as there are so many spellings: *kanafeh, kenafeh, kunafeh* . . . but always pronounced: *kuh-NAF-ee*). This recipe is most similar to the knafeh I've had at Lebanese bakeries, with a finely textured crust and melting cheese layer, which is best eaten warm. I like my knafeh thick, gooey, and salty-sweet. Traditionally knafeh is eaten for breakfast or a snack, and it is often tucked into a version of *ka'ik* that is a savory sesame bread. (There's a sweet version on page 176.) The *ackawi* cheese called for here is a white, firm Arabic cheese that can be found in Middle Eastern markets; a comparable cheese for this is shredded mozzarella. See more about *kataifi* dough on page 20, and where to buy it in Sources, page 243.

Makes 10 servings

- ½ pound / 230 g kataifi dough (page 20 and page 240)
- ¾ cup / 12 g panko
- ¾ cup / 180 g clarified butter (page 41), melted
- 1 cup / 240 mL orange blossom syrup, (page 40), chilled, divided
- 1¼ cups / 300 g whole milk
- ⅓ cup / 50 g fine semolina
- 8 ounces / 230 g ackawi or mozzarella cheese, shredded
- ¼ cup / 40 g finely chopped pistachios, for serving

Preheat the oven to 350°F / 175°C with a rack in the middle position.

In the food processor, pulse the kataifi dough for about 30 seconds, or until it forms a fine meal. Transfer the kataifi to a medium bowl with the panko. Pour the melted butter and ½ cup / 120 mL of orange blossom syrup over the kataifi and stir until the mixture is completely coated.

Press the dough mixture very firmly into the bottom of a 9-inch / 23 cm cake pan, using the flat bottom of a cup or something similar to compress it tightly.

In a small heavy saucepan, heat the milk over medium-high heat until it is hot and steaming, but not boiling. Reduce the heat to medium-low, add the semolina and stir constantly until the mixture is slightly thickened, about 1 minute. Remove the pan from the heat and stir in the cheese.

Pour the cheese mixture over the kataifi in the pan and smooth the top. Bake the knafeh for 40 minutes, or until the cheesy top is light golden brown. Remove the pan from the oven and cool for 15 minutes.

Turn the knafeh out onto a platter with the cheese-side down, and drizzle the top with ¼ cup / 60 mL of the orange blossom syrup. Garnish the top decoratively with pistachio nuts. Serve squares or slices of knafeh warm, with a spoonful of the remaining syrup on each plate.

Mandarin Orange Frozen Yogurt

Frozen yogurt was my father's go-to treat when it first became popular back in the '80s. He loved ice cream with a passion (and passed that on to me), so when he wanted to lower the fat quotient, frozen yogurt was the ticket. I ate a lot of frozen yogurt right along with him, and loved it for its tang—for me, the affinity had nothing to do with low-fat. My version of frozen yogurt also has nothing to do with low-fat (though you can certainly make it that way), and everything to do with flavor. Mandarin oranges squeeze so easily and their flavor is the perfect partner when frozen with yogurt and cream: a sweet, tart grown-up creamsicle.

Makes 8 servings

¾ cup / 150 g granulated sugar

1 tablespoon corn syrup

1½ cups / 360 mL mandarin orange juice (from about 12 mandarin oranges), divided

Juice of 1 lemon

1 cup / 230 g whole milk labneh (page 29) or plain, unsweetened whole milk Greek yogurt

3 ounces / 84 g cream cheese, at room temperature

¼ cup / 60 mL heavy whipping cream

In a 2-quart / 2 L saucepan, melt the sugar and corn syrup with 1 cup / 240 mL of the mandarin orange juice over medium heat. Bring to a boil and simmer for 1 minute.

Pour the mixture into a heatproof bowl with the remaining mandarin orange juice and the lemon juice, cool for 10 minutes, and then cover and chill it until it is completely cold. Or, pour the slightly cooled mixture into a heavy-duty plastic freezer bag and immerse it into a bowl of ice water until it is completely cold.

Whisk the labneh and cream cheese very well in a small bowl, until there are no lumps remaining. Slowly whisk in the cream. Chill this mixture for an hour, or until it is completely cold.

One tablespoon at a time, slowly whisk ½ cup / 120 mL of the mandarin orange mixture into the chilled labneh mixture. Continue whisking in the rest of the juice, in a slow, steady stream to avoid lumps from forming. Churn the frozen yogurt base in an ice cream maker according to the manufacturer's instructions.

Chill the frozen yogurt in the freezer in an airtight container for at least 8 hours and up to several weeks.

Nougat Glacé with Sweet Cherries and Candied Almonds

Because Lebanon was a protectorate of France for the better part of the last century, there is wonderful French influence in Lebanese culture, from fashion to language to cuisine. As a devotee of all things pastry, I'm thrilled that French pastry is a part of our culinary history, and that it inspired me to turn to this "frozen nougat" when I looked for a way to make ice cream before I owned an ice cream maker. This semifreddo is made of a frozen mousse-like mixture of meringue and whipped cream. I've studded mine with toasty caramelized almonds . . . but anything goes, especially candied or dried fruits or simple roasted nuts.

Makes 10 servings

For the candied almonds
(optional; substitute plain roasted, salted almonds)

1 cup / 200 g granulated sugar

½ cup / 75 g whole roasted almonds

For the nougat:

2 cups / 475 mL heavy whipping cream, chilled

5 large egg whites, at room temperature

¼ teaspoon cream of tartar

1 cup / 200 g granulated sugar

½ cup / 120 mL cool water

1 teaspoon vanilla extract

1½ cups / 225 g sweet cherries, pitted and coarsely chopped

For the cherry coulis:

2 cups / 300 g fresh sweet cherries, pitted and chopped

½ cup / 100 g granulated sugar

½ cup / 120 mL water

Juice of 1 lemon

Line a 10 x 5-inch / 25 x 13 cm loaf pan with plastic wrap both crosswise and lengthwise, leaving a 2-inch / 5 cm overhang all the way around.

For the nuts, line a sheet pan with a Silpat or waxed paper. In a 2-quart / 2 L heavy saucepan over medium heat, melt the sugar, stirring minimally, until it is completely dissolved, about 3 minutes. Once the sugar melts and is amber-colored, add the almonds and stir constantly, coating the nuts with the caramel and cooking them for about 1 minute. Pour the almonds onto the prepared sheet pan and spread evenly, taking great care because the mixture is extremely hot. Cool completely, and then chop the nuts coarsely, leaving behind any large pieces of hard caramel that don't contain any almonds. Set the nuts aside, as well as the leftover hard caramel pieces (for garnish).

Whip the cream slowly until it turns to soft peaks, about 2 minutes; cover and chill while you make the nougat.

Using an electric mixer, whip the egg whites with the cream of tartar just until soft peaks form, 2 to 3 minutes. Turn off the mixer. In a heavy small saucepan over medium-high heat, combine the sugar and water. Heat the mixture until it reaches the softball stage (230 to 232°F / 110 to 111°C; careful not to go above this temperature or the syrup will be too stiff). Immediately remove the saucepan from the heat. Turn the mixer back on medium-high and slowly pour the syrup in a thin stream into the egg whites while they're beating. Add the vanilla and continue beating for 5 minutes, or until the nougat is very fluffy, glossy, and stiff peaks have formed. Allow the mixture to cool completely to room temperature.

Fold the chilled whipped cream, candied almonds, and cherries gently into the nougat. Scrape the nougat into the prepared loaf pan and smooth the top. Freeze for at least 8 hours.

For the cherry coulis, bring the cherries, sugar, water, and lemon juice to a boil in a small heavy saucepan over medium-high heat. Simmer and stir occasionally for 8 minutes, or until the fruit breaks down (there will still be pieces of fruit), and then remove it from the heat and cool for 5 minutes. Puree the cherry mixture in a blender or food processor. Pour the puree through a fine mesh sieve into a bowl, pressing on the solids to release the juices. Chill.

To serve the nougat glacé, transfer it from the loaf pan (using the plastic wrap overhang) to a serving platter. Spoon some of the coulis on dessert plates. Run a sharp chef's knife under hot water and slice pieces about an inch wide, rinsing the knife after each slice. Place the slices over the coulis on each plate, dust with some of the reserved chopped caramel bits, and serve immediately.

Spiced Sweet Bread with Rose Water Milk Glaze

My Aunt Louise is famous for her version of ka'ik (pronounced KAH-ick), which she dips in a fragrant rose water glaze. Never mind that Louise is also my mother-in-law . . . the "aunt" title was born out of affection rather than blood relation to her family (promise). Her recipe is so coveted that my husband wonders if I married him just so that I could have access to her way with the ka'ik. This mildly sweet, spiced Lebanese bread is baked for holidays, especially Easter. There are many types of ka'ik, from a sesame-coated pocket bread that is stuffed with sweet cheese knafeh (page 171), to a crunchy, biscuit-like ka'ik cookie. As a sweet bread, ka'ik is pressed into wooden molds (see Sources, pages 242 to 243), but the breads can also be decorated by hand with a fork (the old-school way was with a feather quill) and the edges crimped like a pie. The imprint is more distinct with the molds. But as Aunt Louise says, don't get too fancy; the imprint often bakes out anyway! The mahleb (Mah-LEB, pages 20 and 243), from ground cherry pit kernels, imparts an aromatic, almond-like flavor that is distinctively Lebanese.

Makes 18 loaves

For the spiced sweet bread:

1 tablespoon active dry yeast

¼ cup / 60 mL lukewarm water (about 80°F / 25°C)

¾ cup / 150 g granulated sugar, divided

¾ cup / 180 g clarified butter (page 41)

1⅓ cups / 320 mL whole milk

5½ cups / 715 g unbleached all-purpose flour

1 tablespoon freshly ground mahleb (page 20)

2 tablespoons ground anise seed

½ teaspoon grated nutmeg

1 tablespoon sesame seeds

¼ teaspoon kosher salt

1 teaspoon extra-virgin olive oil

For the rose water milk glaze:

1 tablespoon unsalted butter

¼ cup / 60 mL half-and-half

½ cup / 100 g granulated sugar

3 drops rose water

Proof the yeast by dissolving it in the ¼ cup / 60 mL of lukewarm water with a tablespoon of the ¾ cup / 150 g sugar. After about 10 minutes, the yeast will activate, becoming creamy and foamy.

Warm the clarified butter and milk in a small saucepan over low heat or in the microwave, to about 80°F / 27°C.

In the bowl of an electric mixer, or by hand in a large bowl, whisk the remaining sugar, flour, mahleb, anise, nutmeg, sesame seeds, and salt. Using the unattached dough hook, or with a wooden spoon, moisten the dry ingredients with the yeast mixture. Attach the hook and slowly add the butter and milk mixture, mixing on low speed or with the spoon until the dough forms. Increase the speed to medium and knead the dough for 5 minutes, or by hand for 10 minutes.

Lightly oil a large bowl with the olive oil. Place the dough in the bowl and flip it around to coat the dough and the bowl completely with oil. Cover the bowl with plastic wrap, then a clean kitchen towel. Set the dough in a warm spot to rise until it is a little more than doubled, a full 2 hours; I like to use the oven, turned off.

To create a warm setting for the second rise, place a clean kitchen towel on the counter and cover it with plastic wrap. Pull off handfuls of dough and roll them into 2½-inch / 7 cm balls. Place the balls on the plastic-covered towel about 2 inches / 5 cm apart, and then cover with more plastic wrap and another towel. Let the dough balls rise for 30 minutes.

Place a rack in the center of the oven, and heat the oven to 325°F / 165°C. If you're using a ka'ik mold, press a ball of dough into the mold firmly with the palm of your hand. Carefully remove the dough and place it on an ungreased sheet pan, decorated-side facing up. Repeat this process with the remaining dough, baking 6 at a time and spacing them 2 inches / 5 cm apart. If you're using your hands to shape the dough, flatten each ball with the palm of your hand. Pinch the edges evenly in five or six places, and poke the top with the tines of a fork decoratively. Bake one sheet pan at a time for about 25 minutes, or until the little loaves are golden brown.

Make the glaze while the bread bakes so that you can dip the loaves while they are still warm. Heat the butter, half-and-half, and sugar in a small saucepan over medium heat. Simmer for 1 minute, and then remove from the heat and add the rose water. Pour the glaze into a shallow dish wide enough to dip the bread in. Dip the top of each sweet bread into the glaze when they come out of the oven, placing them on a wire rack to dry.

The ka'ik will keep in an airtight container for several days at room temperature. Eat them at room temperature or warm them in a 250°F / 120°C oven.

Sugared Anise Donuts

Baking days always started with my grandmother, my Sitto, spending the night so that she and my mother could put the dough up to rise in the early morning hours. The days ended with a big plate of sugared donuts, fried with the "leftover" dough (really we just set dough aside for this specific purpose, wanting to be sure there would be enough to fry at the end of the day). What a feast those days were, when we would eat Sitto's Lebanese breads and donuts to our hearts' content. Lebanese donuts, or *zalabia* (zuh-LAY-bee-yuh), are a tradition for the feast of Epiphany in January, but we never waited until then for ours. Zalabia are typically dipped in orange blossom syrup hot out of the oil, but my mom and Sitto always sugared theirs instead, and that's how I love them. The donuts are best eaten warm, immediately after they are fried. A cup of thick, cinnamon-spiced hot chocolate (page 236) alongside doesn't hurt anything, either.

Makes about one dozen

1 tablespoon active dry yeast

1 cup / 240 mL lukewarm water (about 80°F / 27°C), divided, plus more as needed

½ cup / 100 g plus 1 teaspoon granulated sugar, divided

3 cups / 390 g unbleached all-purpose flour

2 teaspoons ground anise seed

1 teaspoon freshly ground mahleb (page 20)

1 teaspoon kosher salt

⅓ cup / 80 mL neutral oil, such as canola or safflower, plus more for frying

Proof the yeast by dissolving it in ¼ cup / 60 mL of the warm water with the teaspoon of sugar. After about 10 minutes, the yeast will activate, becoming creamy and foamy.

Whisk the flour with the ground anise seed, mahleb, and salt in the bowl of an electric mixer or other medium bowl if you're mixing by hand. Moisten the flour by working in the yeast mixture, ½ cup / 120 mL of the warm water, and ⅓ cup of oil using the unattached dough hook from the mixer, or your hands. Attach the dough hook. Mix the dough on medium speed, or by hand, slowly working in the remaining water gradually. Add

additional water by the tablespoon as needed to create a wet, sticky dough.

Knead the dough in the mixer for about 3 minutes or by hand for about 5 minutes until it is very soft and smooth. The dough should still be sticky at this point, but not so much that it leaves dough on your fingers when touched. Kneading by hand can be awkward at first because the dough is so wet, but as you knead, the dough will firm up and absorb all of the water. Sprinkle the dough with a little flour if that's helpful.

Pour a teaspoon of oil into a medium bowl. Flip the dough around the bowl to coat it and the sides of the bowl with the oil completely. Cover the bowl with plastic wrap and then a clean kitchen towel. Place it in a warm spot to rise; I like to use the oven, turned off. Let the dough rise until doubled, about 90 minutes.

Divide the dough into 12 pieces, roll them into balls, and place them about 2 inches / 5 cm apart on a lightly floured work surface. Let them rise, covered with plastic wrap and a kitchen towel, for 20 minutes.

Fill a medium sauté pan or stockpot with high sides with enough of the neutral oil to reach a couple of inches up the sides. Heat the oil over medium-high heat to 350°F / 175°C, or until a tiny ball of dough placed in the oil bubbles up vigorously and immediately. Be careful not to overheat the oil, or the donuts will brown too quickly and will not cook through inside.

Working in batches, stretch 2 or 3 balls of dough into rustic, flat, oblong shapes, and poke a hole in the middle with your thumbs as you stretch. Fry the donuts for about 3 minutes, turning them over halfway through cooking with tongs when they are golden brown. Transfer the donuts to a plate lined with paper towels. Sprinkle them right away with sugar on both sides, and eat them as soon as they are cool enough to bite into. Fry the remaining donuts in the same way.

Variation: Anise Donuts with Orange Blossom Syrup

To glaze the zalabia with orange blossom syrup rather than dusting them with sugar, prepare 1 recipe of the Flower Water Syrup (page 40) with orange blossom water, and set aside. After the first rise divide the dough into 18 pieces, roll them into balls and place them about 2 inches / 5 cm apart on a lightly floured work surface. Let them rise, covered with plastic wrap and a kitchen towel, for 20 minutes. Fry the donuts as directed. Transfer them to a plate lined with paper towels for just a minute to drain, then dip them immediately into orange blossom syrup.

Pastry and Sweets

Labneh with Orange, Avocado, Pomegranate, and Honey

I had to have been well into my 20s before I ate sweet yogurt of any kind. Yogurt was always a savory food in my book; my way of ramping up a bowl of yogurt was with a little salt and pepper, not anything sweet. So the commercial yogurts and their stir-in, jam-like fruits never appealed—but having a giant sweet tooth, I eventually settled into making my bowls of yogurt like this one, sweetened with fresh fruit contrasted with the savory, silky touch of avocado and the tart crunch of pomegranate seeds.

Makes 4 servings

2 cups / 460 g labneh (page 29), or substitute Greek yogurt

2 teaspoons cold water

1 navel orange

1 semi-ripe avocado

Squeeze of fresh lemon juice

1 tablespoon honey

2 tablespoons pomegranate seeds (page 66)

In a small bowl, whisk the labneh with 2 teaspoons of cold water until it is loose and creamy. Spoon the labneh into four small serving bowls.

Peel the orange and cut out the segments. Top the labneh with the segments.

Cut the avocado into 1-inch / 2.5 cm pieces and toss with a squeeze of lemon juice. Top the labneh and orange with the avocado.

Drizzle the honey over the bowls of labneh, orange, and avocado, sprinkle with the pomegranate seeds, and serve.

Labneh with Tart Cherry-Rose Water Compote

Tart cherries are the pride of where I live in northern Michigan, and I'm like a proud parent when it comes to all things Michigan. I want to show her off as though she is mine, as though I did something to make her all that she is. I suppose I love my state the way some love their sports teams; they have a loyalty that won't quit, and when their team wins, so do they personally. There is nothing that expresses Michigan better than our cherries (move over Motor City!); the majority of the nation's tart cherries come from the Great Lakes State, and I don't mind saying just how great they are. Tart cherries are a super food extraordinaire, and eaten dried they are a real Lebanese-style dried fruit treat: sweet-tart, chewy, and, if you're from around these parts, homegrown. I love how the tartness of the dried cherries balances the sweetness of a compote gently fragrant with rose water, so good spooned over a creamy bowl of labneh.

Makes 4 servings

½ cup / 100 g granulated sugar

1 cup / 240 mL plus 2 teaspoons water, divided

¾ cup / 110 g dried cherries

3 drops rose water

2 cups / 460 g labneh (page 29), or substitute Greek yogurt

¼ cup / 40 g toasted walnut halves, coarsely chopped

Grated zest of 1 organic lime

Dissolve the sugar and 1 cup /240 mL of the water in a small saucepan over medium heat. Add the cherries and bring them to a boil. Reduce the heat to medium-low and simmer until the liquid reduces by half, about 15 minutes. Stir in the rose water, and cool the mixture to room temperature.

In a small bowl, whisk the labneh with the remaining 2 teaspoons of water. Spoon the labneh into four small serving bowls.

Top the labneh with the compote, garnish with the toasted walnuts and lime zest, and serve immediately.

Stone Fruit with Flower Waters and Shaved Coconut

It's true that while there is so much to love about Lebanese pastry and sweets, no meal ends at the Lebanese table without a beautiful display of fresh, ripe fruit. I've heard countless stories of how my grandmother Nabeha bragged about the big, voluptuous, sweet fruit of her native Lebanon. Peaches as big as your hand! Lemons the size of a melon! It's hard to know if this was nostalgia or reality talking, but no doubt it was all of the fruits of home, physical, spiritual, and emotional, that reigned large in her memory.

Makes 8 servings

3 pounds / 1.5 kg assorted ripe stone fruits, such as peaches, nectarines, plums, apricots, and cherries

Juice of 2 lemons

2 teaspoons raw creamed honey

1 teaspoon orange blossom water

3 drops rose water

¼ cup / 20 g unsweetened shaved coconut

¼ cup / 50 g pomegranate seeds (page 66)

Split and remove the pits from the fruit, and then slice the halves into 2-inch wedges. For cherries, leave them halved.

In a small bowl, whisk the lemon juice into the honey until it dissolves. Add the orange blossom water and rose water. Taste, and add more of either of the floral waters if needed.

Arrange the fruit on a serving platter or in a serving bowl. Pour the dressing evenly over the fruit. Sprinkle with the shaved coconut and pomegranate seeds, and serve immediately.

Breads & Savory Pies

Talami Sesame Loaves

This Lebanese bread is made with an unusually wet dough, which creates a large, soft crumb and a tender crust. There are a few things that assist in making excellent *talami* (tuh-LAM-ee): Let the dough rise for the second time on well-oiled sheets of plastic wrap, and shape the droopy dough both for the second rise and just before placing it on a hot sheet pan into the oven. You'll need a spray bottle to spritz the dough with water to adhere the sesame seeds to the crust. Because the dough is so wet, it comes together the easiest in an electric mixer, but it can also be made by hand. Talami is delicious eaten warm, at room temperature, or sliced and toasted, spread with labneh and apricot preserves (page 218).

Makes 2 (10-inch) loaves

- 1 tablespoon active dry yeast
- 2¼ cups / 540 mL lukewarm water (about 80°F / 27°C), divided
- 2 tablespoons granulated sugar, divided
- 4 cups / 520 g unbleached all-purpose flour
- ½ tablespoon kosher salt
- ¾ cup / 180 mL neutral oil, such as canola or safflower, divided
- 2 tablespoons toasted sesame seeds (page 32)

Proof the yeast by dissolving it in ¼ cup / 60 mL of the warm water with 1 tablespoon of the sugar. After about 10 minutes, the yeast will activate, becoming creamy and foamy.

Whisk the flour with the remaining sugar and salt in the bowl of an electric mixer or other large bowl if you're mixing by hand. Moisten the flour with the yeast mixture, plus 1 additional cup / 240 mL of the warm water, using the unattached dough hook from the mixer or your hands. Attach the dough hook and turn the mixer on low.

Slowly add ¾ of the remaining cup / 180 mL of warm water, mixing thoroughly after each addition on medium speed. The dough will be wet and almost batter-like; keep mixing for about 5 minutes, adding the remaining ¼ cup / 60 mL of water a little at a time until a very soft dough forms. The talami dough does not look or feel like typical bread dough; it is very droopy and moist, and must be kneaded in the bowl. Knead the dough by hand for a few minutes, until few lumps remain and the dough is moist and smooth. Coat the bowl with 1 tablespoon of the oil by pulling the dough in at the edges and pouring the oil under it there, rubbing the oil all around the bowl under the dough, over the top of the dough, and up the sides of the bowl.

Cover the bowl with plastic wrap, without letting it touch the dough. Cover that with a towel and place the bowl in a warm spot to rise; I like to use the oven, turned off or on the proof setting if you have it. Allow the dough to rise for about 90 minutes, or until the dough is doubled.

Line the kitchen counter with 4 sheets of plastic wrap about 18 inches / 46 cm long, overlapping the sheets so the oil won't seep through. Coat the wrap generously with half of the remaining oil.

Taking care not to disturb too many of the bubbly air pockets in the dough, gently pull half of the dough from the bowl and shape it into a ball; lay it on the prepared plastic wrap. Do the same with the other half of the dough, placing it several inches from the first to leave room for the second rise. The dough will be quite soft and droopy, and may not form a perfectly round shape at this stage. Gently rub the dough generously with more oil, coating the entire surface of the dough, and let them rise for 30 minutes.

Meanwhile, arrange the rack in the center of the oven and place a heavy rimmed sheet pan in the oven. Heat the oven to 400°F / 200°C (for convection, 375°F / 190°C).

Remove the hot pan from the oven. Lift one of the risen dough balls (it will have settled into a flatter shape) and shape it into a taller ball. Place the ball in the center of the pan. Use a spray bottle of lukewarm water to lightly spray the surface of the dough. Sprinkle the top liberally with sesame seeds, and press them down into the dough lightly with the tips of your fingers.

Bake the talami for about 10 to 15 minutes (convection bakes faster than standard oven heat, so it will be on the shorter end of the range), or until the loaf is light golden brown. If further browning is needed, place the bread under the broiler briefly. Remove from the oven and cool the loaf on a wire rack for at least 15 minutes before slicing. Bake the second loaf the same way.

Store the cooled bread wrapped thoroughly in plastic at room temperature for 2 days, in the refrigerator for a few days, or in the freezer for several months.

MY MAN'OUSHE MISSION

My brother Chris was the first to speak to me of the *man'oushe*. Every time he returned from a trip to Lebanon, I wanted to sit him down and discuss, in detail, every bite of food he'd eaten. He was happy to oblige, but nothing he described, even the elaborate meals with family and more family, made his eyes go wide like the man'oushe. It's street corner bakery food, he said. You get it wrapped in paper and off you go. They'd stopped on a whim because they were hungry and needed a snack, and it turned out to be the best Lebanese food he'd ever put in his mouth. The flatbread was chewy, but with a crisp exterior. It was blistered (okay, my word, not his) and warm, topped with za'atar or cheese, filled with tomatoes and pink pickled turnips and mint and folded over on itself.

I had to stop him. I couldn't take it.

Breads like this were not unfamiliar to me; I'd had them before. But those were breads that came in plastic bags.

No matter how fresh they say the bread is, it's still bread that you get in a plastic bag. Warm-from-the-oven man'oushe is something bread-dreams are made of, something you are only going to get from your own kitchen.

To say my list of must-eat foods was lengthy when I visited Lebanon myself is an understatement. So when Day 2 of the trip commenced and I still hadn't eaten my man'oushe, I began to feel anxious. We started the day with breakfast in the hotel, which was a beautiful breakfast to behold, but not a man'oushe breakfast.

Our first stop that day was American University at Beirut, an oasis in the city surrounded by a stone wall and plenty of security. Stepping through the gates and onto the quad on that sunny morning took my breath away—for the views out over the sea, for the architecture and the massive trees everywhere, for the thoughts of my great uncle, a dean at the school who had kept a correspondence with my father long ago.

But also, and perhaps primarily, I found the students breathtaking. I have never been in a place where most everyone looks like a cousin, or a sister, or . . . me. And there, through the window of an unreachable student union building, I saw rows and rows of man'oushe waiting for the students to scoop them up to have with their orange juice, sustenance for the day.

By the time we reached our next destination to meet our family in the village of El Mtein, I thought man'oushe would have to be tabled to a Day 3 obsession. Then my cousin suggested an out-of-the-way place for lunch, up even higher in the hills, a casual spot whose specialty is a very flat, God bless it, man'oushe.

It's his favorite, he said, his very favorite food to eat. Our bread there was topped with the classic *kwarma*, preserved lamb, confit-style; we also had labneh and cheese on our breads, and alongside there were chickpeas and fava beans doused in good olive oil, black olives, and the requisite whole tomatoes, cucumbers, onions, and mint.

Holy Grail. Holy day. Holy moly. I vowed I would learn that bread, and that day came one snowy winter morning when I was back up north in Michigan. Under the guidebook of Barbara Abdeni Massaad, a devotee who wrote and photographed an entire beautiful book about Lebanese man'oushe, I've been turning breads out in the kind of feverish excitement that comes with reaching the summit of one's quest. I had to call my brother and tell him about the chewiness, the blistering beauty, the za'atar warm from the oven.

But he had to stop me. He just couldn't take it.

Za'atar Flatbread

Fresh-baked flatbread coated with za'atar and olive oil, known as *man'oushe* (mahn-OOH-shee), is the quintessential breakfast food in Lebanon, and on Lebanese tables all over the world. When I made my first trip to Lebanon, I watched with fascination as everyone walked around with their morning za'atar bread, rolled up in paper for breakfast on the run from the corner bakeries. I'll take that over my plain old granola bar for breakfast any day! I am a grateful apprentice to Barbara Abdeni Massaad's wonderful book *Man'oushe: Inside the Street Corner Lebanese Bakery* (Interlink 2013), and this recipe is based on hers. Your own homemade za'atar flatbread, warm from the oven, is a pleasure so worth having. The dough can be made by hand, but I find the dough dramatically more beautiful, softer, and stickier made in the food processor fitted with the metal blade. (As with pizza dough, a soft and sticky dough makes a better flatbread.) Try rolling the man'oushe up with a stuffing of pink pickled turnips (page 206), cucumbers, onions, arugula, and labneh, or just eat the accompaniments with slices of the bread.

Makes 4 (10-inch / 25 cm) flatbreads

- 1 teaspoon active dry yeast
- 1¼ cups / 300 mL lukewarm water (about 80°F / 27°C), divided
- 1 tablespoon granulated sugar
- 2½ cups / 325 g unbleached all-purpose flour, plus more as needed
- 1 cup / 130 g cake flour
- 2 teaspoons kosher salt
- 1 tablespoon neutral oil, such as canola or safflower
- ½ cup / 120 mL plus 1 teaspoon extra-virgin olive oil, divided
- ½ cup / 45 g za'atar

Proof the yeast by dissolving it in ¼ cup / 60 mL of the warm water with the sugar. After about 10 minutes, the yeast will activate, becoming creamy and foamy.

Pulse the flours and salt in the bowl of the food processor. Add the tablespoon of neutral oil and the yeast mixture to the processor, and with the processor running, slowly add the remaining cup of warm water and process for 1 minute. The dough will form a ball and turn in the bowl as the machine runs.

Alternatively, to use the electric mixer or your hands, work the yeast mixture and neutral oil into the flours and salt using the unattached dough hook from the mixer, or your hands. Slowly add ½ cup / 120 mL of the warm water. Attach the dough hook and mix the dough on medium speed, or by hand, slowly working in the remaining ½ cup / 120 mL of warm water. Mix or knead until the dough is soft and smooth, about 3 minutes.

Pour a teaspoon of the olive oil into a clean medium bowl. Add the dough and flip it around the bowl to coat it and the sides of the bowl with the oil. Cover the bowl completely with plastic wrap, without letting the wrap touch the dough. Cover that with a clean kitchen towel and place the bowl in a warm spot to rise; I like to use the oven (off, or with the proof setting on, if you have it). Let the dough rise until doubled in size, up to 90 minutes.

Divide the dough into four evenly sized balls. Set them on a lightly floured surface and coat them lightly with more all-purpose flour. Cover the balls with the plastic wrap and kitchen towel and let rise for 20 minutes.

Meanwhile, heat a baking stone in the oven. Place the stone or an overturned heavy sheet pan in the lower third of the oven (it's overturned so the edges won't get in the way of placing and removing the dough). Remove the racks above it to clear space for moving the bread in and out, and heat the oven to 425°F / 220°C for 20 to 30 minutes. Convection baking is ideal here, if possible. If you're using convection, set the oven temperature to 400°F / 200°C.

In a small bowl, combine the za'atar and the remaining olive oil to form a wet paste, stirring well. Set aside.

To roll out the dough, lightly flour the work surface, a rolling pin, and a peel (or another overturned sheet pan to be used as a peel, like a huge spatula). The flour acts as ball bearings for the dough to prevent it from sticking to surfaces. Place one ball of dough on the floured surface and press down on it with the palm of your hand. The key to getting the dough rolled flat and round is to keep it moving, which means turning it frequently throughout the rolling process and adding more flour lightly to the work surface as you go. Roll the dough from the center of the circle all the way out to the edge a couple of times, rotate it, and then roll again, repeating until the dough is about 8 inches / 20 cm across and ¼ inch / .5 cm thick.

Flour the peel and, using two hands to help the dough keep its shape, slide the rolled dough onto it. Spread 3 teaspoons of the za'atar paste on the dough using the back of the spoon or your fingertips to get an even, thick spread. Leave a ½-inch / 1.5 cm rim around the edge of the dough. Shake the peel back and forth to be sure the dough will move off of it into the oven, and if it doesn't move easily, lift the edges and dash more flour underneath. Slide the dough onto the hot baking stone or pan and bake for 7 to 10 minutes.

You'll want to keep the oven light on to watch the beautiful, bubbling baking show that goes on while the bread bakes. When the bread has formed many air pockets and is golden brown at the edges, remove it from the oven to a baking rack and cool for a few minutes. The za'atar topping may seem oily when it's still hot out of the oven, but it will dry as it cools and taste just right. Repeat the process with the rest of the balls of dough, rolling the next one out while another loaf finishes baking in the oven. Eat the bread warm on its own or with accompaniments.

Store the bread, well wrapped with plastic, in the refrigerator for a few days, in the freezer for a few months, or at room temperature for a couple of days.

Homemade Pita Bread

Homemade pita is more rustic and slightly thicker than the traditional, very thin Lebanese pita that's made so by special equipment in a professional bakery. That exact thinness just can't be achieved at home—I am assured by every professional pita baker I've known, and by my own countless not-so-thin attempts. Still, it's a lot of fun to watch your own pita puff up in the oven, and to enjoy it fresh and warm at home from your own hands. One of the Lebanese bread bakers I know in Chicago, a thin, beautiful woman, told me she finds pita bread is so healthy and good, she could "eat the bread wrapped in the bread!" I make pita dough in the food processor, but you will also have success with the mixer or by hand.

Makes 8 (8-inch / 30 cm) pitas

- 1 teaspoon active dry yeast
- 1¼ cups / 300 mL lukewarm water (about 80°F / 27°C), divided
- 1 tablespoon granulated sugar
- ¼ cup / 35 g whole wheat flour
- 1¾ cups / 228 g unbleached all-purpose flour
- 1½ cups / 195 g cake flour
- 1 teaspoon kosher salt
- 1 tablespoon plus 1 teaspoon neutral oil, such as canola or safflower, divided

Proof the yeast by dissolving it in ¼ cup / 60 mL of the warm water with the sugar and whole wheat flour. After about 10 minutes, the yeast will activate, becoming creamy and foamy.

Pulse the all-purpose and cake flours with the salt in the bowl of the food processor. Add the 1 tablespoon of oil and the yeast mixture, and with the processor running, slowly add the remaining cup / 240 mL of warm water and process for 1 minute. The dough will form a ball and turn in the bowl as the machine runs.

To use the electric mixer or your hands rather than the processor, work the proofed yeast and oil into the flours and salt using the unattached dough hook for the mixer, or your hands. Slowly add ½ cup / 120 mL of the warm water. Attach the dough hook and mix the dough on medium speed, or by hand, slowly working in the remaining ½ cup / 120 mL of warm water. Mix or knead until the

dough is soft and smooth, about 3 minutes.

Pour the teaspoon of oil into a clean medium bowl. Shape the dough into a ball, and flip the dough around in the bowl to coat it and the sides of the bowl with the oil. Cover the bowl completely with plastic wrap, without letting the wrap touch the dough. Cover that with a clean kitchen towel and place in a warm, draft-free environment. Let the dough rise until doubled in size, up to 90 minutes.

Place a baking stone or an overturned heavy sheet pan in the center of the oven with the racks above it removed, and preheat the oven to 550°F / 288°C (for convection, heat to 525°F / 274°C).

Deflate the dough by gently pushing it down, and then cover it again and let it rest another 10 minutes. Shape the dough into a log on a lightly floured work surface and divide it in half, and then divide each half into 4 pieces for a total of 8 pieces. Shape each piece into a ball and place them about 3 inches / 7.5 cm apart on a lightly floured work surface. Cover with plastic wrap to rest for 30 minutes.

The dough is rolled out twice, in order to get the thinnest possible pita. Clear a workspace large enough to set aside the rounds of dough after they have been rolled out to about 8-inch / 20 cm rounds. Very lightly flour the work surface (too much flour makes the dough more difficult to roll out; a little stickiness is a good thing). Roll the dough from the center of the circle to the edge a couple of times, rotate it, and then roll again, repeating until the dough is 6 to 8 inches / 15 to 20 cm across and ¼ inch / .5 cm thick.

Carefully move the rolled dough to a lightly floured work surface to rest, covered with plastic, for 5 minutes. Roll the dough out again on a very lightly floured, somewhat sticky work surface.

To bake the bread, lightly flour the peel to transfer the dough to the hot stone in the oven after its second roll-out, or use an overturned sheet pan. Shake the peel back and forth to be sure that the dough is loose enough to slide off of it into the oven. Bake each pita separately, rolling another one out while the one in the oven bakes. Bake the bread until it puffs up and turns light golden brown (some spots will blister and brown), about 3 minutes. Remove the bread from the oven with the peel.

The puffed-up loaves are hollow and hard at first. Very lightly spritz the tops of the loaves with water when they come out of the oven, and allow them to cool for about 10 minutes. Flatten the pitas and place them in airtight plastic bags immediately so that they stay soft. Store the bread in the refrigerator for up to 5 days, or in the freezer for several months.

Variation: Pita Wrap

Pitas make a fantastic wrap for just about anything you have on hand: summer vegetables, scallions, olives, pickles, toasted nuts, herbs, and leftover meats. My favorite iteration is this: 1 large thin pita piled with a big dollop of labneh, cucumber spears, a sliced tomato, sliced sweet onion, arugula, and pickled turnip (page 206), drizzled with olive or pistachio oil and red or white wine vinegar. Don't forget to season with salt and pepper. Roll the pita up, and you're ready to eat. Cut the wrap in half on an angle, crosswise, when you want to be extra-civilized. If you're not eating the pita wrap immediately, wrap it up in plastic to keep the bread soft. (If you're using thicker pita, like homemade, open the pita up and place the fillings inside.) This was my favorite brown bag lunch to take to work with me when I lived in Chicago. Pita wraps made my co-workers jealous, and they sure beat the repetitive salad-and-sandwich eating.

Breads and Savory Pies

Savory Pie Dough

The special thing about this dough is its suppleness, which allows for the dough to be rolled out thinly and to bake up that way too. This makes for a thinner, more delicate pouch for fillings like spinach (page 198), lamb (page 201), or labneh (page 203), which is so much better than the doughy versions typical of commercial Middle Eastern bakeries. I like to make this dough in the electric mixer fitted with the dough hook, but you will have success by hand as well.

Makes dough for about 30 hand pies

- 1 tablespoon active dry yeast
- 1 cup / 240 mL lukewarm water (about 80°F / 27°C), divided, plus more as needed
- 1 teaspoon granulated sugar
- 3 cups / 390 g unbleached all-purpose flour
- 1 teaspoon kosher salt
- ⅓ cup / 80 mL plus 1 teaspoon neutral oil, such as canola or safflower, divided

Proof the yeast by dissolving it in ¼ cup / 60 mL of the warm water with the sugar. After about 10 minutes, the yeast will activate, becoming creamy and foamy.

Whisk the flour with the salt in the bowl of an electric mixer or other medium bowl if you're mixing by hand. Moisten the flour with the yeast mixture, ⅓ cup / 80 mL of the oil, and ½ cup / 120 mL of the warm water using the unattached dough hook from the mixer, or your hands. Attach the dough hook and mix the dough on medium speed, or by hand, slowly working in the remaining water, adding just enough to create a wet, sticky dough. Add more water a tablespoon at a time if needed.

Knead the dough in the mixer for 3 minutes or by hand for 5 minutes, or until it is very soft and smooth. The dough should still be quite sticky at this point, but not so much that it leaves dough on your fingers when touched. Kneading by hand can be awkward at first because the dough is so wet, but as you knead, the dough will firm up and absorb much of the moisture. Sprinkle the dough with a little flour if that's helpful as you knead it.

Pour the remaining teaspoon of oil into a medium bowl. Shape the dough into a ball, and flip the dough around the bowl to coat it and the sides of the bowl with the oil. Cover the bowl with plastic wrap (without letting the wrap touch the dough), then with a clean kitchen towel, and place the bowl in a warm spot to rise; I like to use the oven, turned off. Let the dough rise until doubled, about 60 to 90 minutes. Avoid a rise much longer than this, or the dough becomes too spongy for the thin crust we're after for the pies. Make the pie filling as directed in any of the savory pie recipes while the dough rises.

Roll half of the dough on an unfloured work surface, rotating often, to about 15 inches / 38 cm across and ⅛ inch / 3 mm thick, keeping the remaining half covered in the bowl. Gently lift up the dough by the edges, lifting all the way to the center of the rolled dough, so the dough can contract before you cut out the rounds. Roll again and lift again. Cut the dough into 3½-inch / 9 cm rounds, cutting the circles as close together as possible so that most of the dough is used up (a second roll out is possible but the dough does not roll or bake up as nicely the second time around). Knead together the scraps, place them back in the bowl next to the remaining dough, and cover the bowl with plastic.

At this point, you can use the dough circles as directed for any of the pie recipes, and you'll roll out the remaining dough (roll the scrap dough separately from the unused dough) while the first batch is baking.

Spinach Pies (triangle-shaped) page 198, and Ba'albek Sfeha (open-faced square), page 201

Spinach Pies

When Dan and I were dating long distance, I always welcomed him on his visits Up North with these golden little spinach pies, these fatayar (fuh-TIE-ah). He spent the trip thinking as much (or more?) about the fatayar awaiting him as he did our visit, and I spent the afternoon of his arrival making dough, forming the triangles, and baking as many as I could. When he arrived, I had to stop him from eating every last one of them warm from the oven—I wanted there to be enough left to send with him on his trip home, since fatayar make such great road trip and picnic food too. Here's my perfected recipe for a batch of fatayar, a great way to welcome someone special through your door, or to send them off.

Makes about 30 pies

1 recipe savory pie dough (page 195)

2 packages (20 ounces / 565 g) frozen chopped spinach, thawed and drained

1 medium-size sweet onion, finely diced

1 teaspoon kosher salt

Juice of 1 lemon

¼ teaspoon ground cinnamon

¼ teaspoon ground allspice

Few grinds of black pepper

⅓ cup / 50 g toasted pine nuts or chopped toasted walnuts

¼ cup / 60 mL extra-virgin olive oil, plus more as needed for coating pies

While the dough is rising, make the filling. Firmly squeeze out any juice from the thawed spinach. The goal is to make the spinach as dry as possible so that its juices, when baked, won't cause the fatayar triangles to open up at the seams. Combine the spinach and onion in a medium bowl. Add the salt, lemon juice, cinnamon, allspice, and pepper and stir thoroughly. Taste and adjust the seasonings until the spinach and onions taste well-seasoned and delicious.

To fill and bake the fatayar, place a rack in the center of the oven, and heat the oven to 375°F / 190°C. Line two heavy baking sheets with foil and brush each one with 2 tablespoons of the olive oil.

Place a heaping tablespoon of filling in the center of each 3½-inch / 9 cm circle that has been cut from the dough. Be careful not to let the filling touch the edges of the dough, or their seams won't stick together well. A good way to keep the filling in the center is to use your fingertips to place and position it. Drop a few of the toasted nuts on top.

Pull up three opposite sides of the dough together in the center over the spinach and pinch it firmly there. Continue pinching the dough together firmly along the three seams to close them, doing this a couple of times to strengthen the seal and gently massaging the pie into a triangle as you pinch. Do the same for each pie, placing them on the prepared sheet pans as you go, and stopping to bake one pan when it is full.

Before baking, generously brush or rub the exterior of each fatayar with olive oil. Bake one pan of fatayar for 12 to 15 minutes, or until the pies are light golden brown. Brush the tops of the fatayar lightly with olive oil again immediately after removing them from the oven.

Make the second pan of pies while the first one bakes, rolling and cutting the dough as directed in the savory pie dough recipe (page 195). Knead the dough scraps and let them rest, covered, for a few minutes before rolling them all out together for a final batch.

Serve the fatayar warm or at room temperature. They freeze perfectly in a freezer bag for up to 6 months, reheated directly from the freezer to the oven at 350°F / 175 °C until warmed through.

IT TAKES A (LEBANESE) VILLAGE

I was sitting in the back seat of the car, mumbling about the fact that I had not seen much kibbeh nayeh (KIB-bee NIGH-yah) on the menus in restaurants during my first days of my first visit to Beirut. That's when Hisam, our driver (which one needs in Lebanon as a tourist, or at least I sure did), pulled out his phone and started talking a mile a minute in Arabic. His animation captured my attention so that I stopped what I was doing and just watched him go. When he hung up, he said it was settled: we would stop for lunch at the home of his sister in Ba'albek, who makes the finest raw kibbeh in all of Lebanon. His expression was so certain, so absolute, that any hesitations I had took a back seat, and I found myself in unison with Hisam, that yes, of course, we must go.

My mother, my sister, and I kept telling ourselves this would be fine, just fine, even as we walked down a dark, uncomfortable hallway in the apartment building to meet Hisam's family. They brought us in and showed us around, and took us right to the table. We sat in a bit of an awkward silence, with their Arabic and our English and the unlikely meeting in their home.

Then platters of food started emerging from the kitchen. The kibbeh, it was exceptional (page 102). But the real standout was the warm, fragrant sfeha, lamb pies delivered in boxes wrapped in newspaper and tied with a string. One of the children ran in with the boxes and put them on the table in what seemed like a regular ritual. Hisam tore open the paper and started lining the sfeha up next to each of our bowls of fattoush (raw vegetables in a foreign land? At that point, having thrown caution to the wind to eat raw kibbeh, you'd better believe we were eating the salad, too). The sfeha meat came from the family butcher at one end of the street; it was seasoned and delivered to the bakery that was situated at the other end of the street. There the bakers rolled, cut, shaped, and baked quantities of the little square sfeha pies for everyone in the village in a massive stone oven. They've been baking sfeha this way, so well and for so many generations, that pies of this sort are known throughout Lebanon as Ba'albek sfeha.

You like them! Hisam announced to us and his sister's family as we ate one after another after another, now speaking a language we all could understand—the language of OH MY!, the language of eyes grown wide with every bite, the language of total communion. Hisam's sister filled our plates with more almost every time we took a bite, a move that reminded me of every Lebanese woman I have ever known, wanting us to eat to our hearts' content.

That day in Lebanon, eating kibbeh, fattoush, and sfeha, was an unforgettable feast, but it was the generous welcome we received in the home of a stranger that showed us the true beauty, language, and flavor of the Lebanese table.

Ba'albek Sfeha
(Open-Faced Lamb Pies)

These succulent pies are similar to fatayar and made with the same dough, but these are open-faced squares. The sfeha meat can also be used to make fatayar-style triangles. Sfeha are best made with a little fat in the meat, so that the juices cook into the dough, flavoring it wonderfully.

Makes about 30 sfeha

1 recipe savory pie dough (page 195)

12 ounces / 340 g coarse-ground leg of lamb (substitute beef chuck, 80 percent lean)

1½ teaspoons kosher salt

2 tablespoons plain, unsweetened yogurt

1 tablespoon pomegranate molasses

¼ teaspoon ground cinnamon

¼ teaspoon ground allspice

1 medium-size sweet onion, finely chopped

2 tablespoons pine nuts, toasted

¼ cup / 60 mL extra-virgin olive oil, plus more as needed for coating pies

⅓ cup / 50 g pomegranate seeds

Recipe Continues On Next Page

Make the filling while the pie dough rises. In a medium mixing bowl, combine the meat, salt, yogurt, pomegranate molasses, cinnamon, all-spice, onion, and pine nuts. Use your hands to combine the meat mixture gently without over-working it, which can make the meat tough.

When the dough is ready, heat the oven to 400°F / 200°C. Line two heavy rimmed sheet pans with foil and brush them each with 2 tablespoons of the olive oil.

Using your fingers or a small spoon, place about a tablespoon of the meat filling in the center of each 3½-inch / 9 cm circle that has been cut from the dough.

Shape the meat pies by using your first finger and thumb of both hands to tightly pinch the dough together on opposite sides of the meat, and then again on the two opposing sides, to form a square around the meat. The sfeha look some-thing like a hamentaschen cookie, but with four sides instead of three.

Press the meat down a little bit to tuck it into the pastry, and continue to pinch the four corners and shape the squares to strengthen the corners for baking, bringing the dough right up next to and slightly over the meat.

Continue shaping each of the pies, placing them on the lined sheet pans as you finish each one. Once a pan is filled with pies spaced about an inch apart, brush or dab each one, dough and meat, with more of the olive oil.

Bake the sfeha for 12 to 15 minutes, or until they are light golden brown and the meat is cooked through.

Make the second pan of pies while the first one bakes; repeat the process of rolling and cutting the dough with the other half, not including the scraps from the first roll out, as directed in the savory pie dough recipe (page 195). Knead the dough scraps and let them rest, covered, for a few minutes before rolling them all out together for a final batch. Fill and form the pies, coat them with oil, and bake as directed above.

When the pies are done baking, sprinkle a few pomegranate seeds on each one and serve them immediately, or hold off on the pomegranate seeds until serving time if you'll be reheating them. Store the pies in an airtight container in the refrigerator for 3 days, or freeze for several months. Reheat the sfeha directly from the refrigerator or freezer in a 350°F / 175°C oven.

Labneh and Mint Pies

Without a doubt, these are my favorite savory pies, which is saying a lot, because they're all so delectable. These are special—and not something anyone in the family made very often, so my discovery of how simple and luxurious the labneh filling is has been that much more exciting. These are shaped as crescents, but they can also be shaped in triangles, like Spinach Pies (page 198).

Makes about 30 pies

¼ cup / 60 mL extra-virgin olive oil, plus more as needed for coating pies

1 cup / 230 g labneh (page 29), or substitute Greek yogurt

2 scallions, finely chopped

1 teaspoon crushed dried mint

5 fresh mint leaves, finely chopped

½ teaspoon kosher salt

1 small garlic clove, minced

1 recipe savory pie dough (page 195)

Line two sheet pans with foil and brush each with 2 tablespoons of the oil. Preheat the oven to 400°F / 200°C.

In a small bowl, stir the labneh, scallions, dried and fresh mint, salt, and garlic until they're well-combined.

Using two small spoons, place about a teaspoon of the labneh filling in the center of each 3½-inch / 9 cm circle that has been cut from the dough. Fold half of the circle over the filling, making a half-moon shape and taking care not to let the edges of the dough touch the labneh, or the dough won't stick together. Press the top layer of dough firmly into the bottom layer along the edge. Crimp this edge decoratively as you would a pie crust, or simply press your fingertip along the curved edge firmly. Place the crescents on one of the prepared sheet pans as you work. To bow the crescent, push the two ends of the crescent away from the crimped edge with one hand while pushing in on the center of the folded side of the crescent with the other hand. Once a pan is filled, brush the crescents lightly with olive oil and bake them until they are golden brown, 12 to 15 minutes. Brush the tops of the crescents lightly with oil again immediately after removing them from the oven.

Make the second pan of pies while the first one bakes by repeating the process of rolling and cutting the dough with the other half, not including the scraps from the first roll out, as directed in the savory pie dough recipe (page 195). Knead the dough scraps and let them to rest, covered, for a few minutes before rolling them all out together for a final batch.

Serve the pies warm or at room temperature. They'll keep in an airtight container in the refrigerator for several days. Or, freeze the baked crescents and reheat from frozen in a 350°F / 175°C oven.

Pickles & Preserves

Lift (Hot Pink Turnip Pickle)

Garlic Mushroom Pickle

Carrot Coriander Pickle

Mixed Pickle Jar

Cauliflower Pepper Pickle

Spiced White Grapes

Fig and Anise Jam with Walnuts

Preserved Watermelon Rind

Apricot Preserves

Apricot-Lime Fruit Leather

All of the pickles and preserves here are "quick," meaning that they should be stored in the refrigerator and eaten within the timeframe specified.

Lift
(Hot Pink Turnip Pickle)

Lift, our ubiquitous hot pink turnip pickles, will last and gain great flavor up to three months, or more, refrigerated. The pickles are so pretty and give great flavor and crunch in or alongside a sandwich, with a hummus (page 49) or baba gannouj (page 68) plate, or served with olives and cocktails. Eat lift with most any Lebanese savory dish you can think of, or as a maza all on their own. Select turnips that are heavy and firm.

Makes 1 quart / 1 L

1 cup / 240 mL distilled white vinegar

½ cup / 120 mL cold water

1½ tablespoons kosher salt

1¼ pounds / 565 g white turnips, trimmed and peeled

1 small beet, trimmed and peeled

1 jalapeño pepper (optional) or 1 teaspoon red pepper flakes (optional)

3 garlic cloves, peeled

1 teaspoon pickling spice

In a small bowl, combine the vinegar, water, and salt to make a brine. Let the mixture sit for a few minutes, stirring occasionally until the salt is dissolved.

Cut the turnips and beet in half from top to bottom, and then into ½-inch- / 1.5 cm thick wedges or slices. Pierce the jalapeño with a knife for mild heat, or cut it in half lengthwise to expose the seeds and ribs for more heat. Pack the turnips and beets into a quart / 1 L jar layered with the garlic cloves, tucking in the hot pepper next to the glass as you go (it's pretty that way), and top with the hot pepper flakes (if using) and the pickling spice.

Pour the brine into the jar, leaving about ½-inch / 1.5 cm headspace. Top the jar with the lid and refrigerate for at least 3 days and up to several months, shaking up the jar occasionally at first to distribute the pink hue of the beet.

DELICIOUS WITHOUT SALT

The Abood sisters, my aunts, had talents. Helen sang like a star, Hilda cooked like magic. When their mother died young at 49, Hilda seized her tasks like a woman who had finally found her mission in life. She would go into the kitchen and heal the family of its loss, and in return would find an essential aspect of her identity.

I remember what's been many years ago now, when she called some of the family over for one of her Lebanese feasts, to give comfort to her brother, my Uncle Fred. He had recently learned he had cancer of the esophagus, a terrible irony for a man who loved food as he did. Aunt Hilda set her defenses against the menace of death as it hovered over the family: prayer and cooking. She began preparing the dinner days ahead, making the laban and pickling the *lift*, Lebanese pink turnips. The shocking pink lift, achieved by a red beet slipped into the jar, calls to mind sugar flowers on a birthday cake, pink bubble gum, or some other unnatural sweet. But these crunchy pickles are strong and piquant beneath their sweet-seeming technicolor, certainly a surprise to an unsuspecting eater. Lift is like the Lebanese themselves, typically well-dressed in unabashed style, and underneath: strength. Edge. And always, piquant humor.

Aunt Hilda's menu that night included so many dishes that they couldn't all fit on the table and sideboard. She rolled one hundred grape leaves cooked with lemon and butter over pork neck bones, roasted two chickens for hushweh, made her kibbeh two ways, *nayeh* and *sahnieh*. There were bowls of romaine with lemon and oil, laban with mint and cucumbers, thickened labneh with olive oil, mashed potatoes, green beans with caramelized onion and toasted almonds, relishes of olives, radishes, peppers. It was a feast for a huge crowd, when in reality we were just eight people. The quantity reflected her gift of love, and the enormity of her pain for her brother, more than her number of guests.

The table was set with Aunt Hilda's good white and gold wedding china. Her house was spotless, her furniture elegant, everything from carpet to couches in white. When the family arrived, they came in through the garage door, which Aunt Hilda liked so she could greet everyone as only she could—and from the moment they stepped out of their cars in her driveway. "You're so delicious," she greeted me, "I could eat you without salt." Each one of us thought we were her favorite.

The men walked through the kitchen and made a little plate of grape leaves to take into the family room for a maza. Aunt Hilda took them tall glasses of ice water. Whenever anyone arrives at the house of an Abood, they are offered, or just handed, a glass of ice water. It's our symbol of hospitality, our pineapple at the door.

When we did eat, it happened quickly: Aunt Hilda said a generous blessing, what a gift it was for her to have us at her house, and we remembered the faithful departed, may they rest in peace. A tearful if brief blessing was made for Uncle Fred's illness. He ate small portions of chicken and grape leaves, and as he ate I saw him stroking Hilda's arm next to him. Uncle Dick piled his plate high; his hunger to satisfy his appetite was second only to his hunger to demonstrate his appreciation for his sister's food. He reached for a radish as he ate— radishes Aunt Hilda had sent me on a special trip to the store to buy earlier that afternoon. "Dick likes those," she said, "and I'm out of them." She and I both saw him take the radish and eat it, and when I looked at her she smiled and winked back to say, "Good thing we got the radishes!"

Then the dance of the leftovers was Hilda's forte: she begged each of us to take kibbeh and grape leaves and hushweh. There was refusal; she reminded us she is alone and can't possibly eat it, it didn't taste good to her, and she doesn't want to eat it again anyway. My mother reminded her that the cook never thinks the food she's been staring at for three days is as good as the guests who come to it fresh. I broke the cycle by saying I'd like to take some of her spicy lift, which was excellent, famously so. Her pleasure was evident as she launched into a litany of all of the people she knows who "rave about it!" When Aunt Pat and Uncle Fred walked out intentionally without leftovers, Aunt Hilda sent me running out to their car with a bundle of grape leaf rolls. "I don't care if he can't eat them," she said. "He loves them, and I just want him to have them."

Garlic Mushroom Pickle

These mushrooms are an absolute favorite for their versatility and mouth-watering umami flavor. The vinaigrette used to pickle the mushrooms and garlic makes a divine dipping oil for good bread. Mound the mushrooms on a small plate with the oil in a small bowl beside it, and a loaf of bread alongside (try them with Talami, page 186, or Homemade Pita Bread, page 192). Make a salad or steamed green beans special by topping them with some of the mushrooms and vinaigrette.

Makes 1 pint

1 pound / 450 g small mushrooms, such as white button

1¼ teaspoons kosher salt, divided

6 cups / 1.5 L warm water

3 garlic cloves, peeled

½ tablespoon whole black peppercorns, cracked

2 sprigs fresh thyme

¼ cup / 60 mL neutral oil, such as safflower or canola

¾ cup / 180 mL white wine vinegar

½ teaspoon dried thyme

Clean and trim the mushrooms. Place them in a 4-quart / 4 L saucepan with 1 teaspoon of the salt and cover them with the warm water. Bring this to a boil, and then reduce the heat to low and simmer for 5 minutes.

Drain the mushrooms in a colander and pat them dry with paper towels. When the mushrooms have cooled off to room temperature, pack them into a clean pint jar with the garlic, peppercorns, and sprigs of fresh thyme.

In a small saucepan, combine the oil, vinegar, dried thyme, and ¼ teaspoon of the salt. Bring the mixture just to a boil over medium heat, and then immediately ladle the hot mixture into the packed jar, leaving ½-inch / 1.5 cm headspace.

Top the jar with the lid and store it in the refrigerator for a few days for the flavors to develop. The mushrooms will keep in the refrigerator for a couple of weeks.

Carrot Coriander Pickle

This pickle is great with cocktails, alongside a sandwich, on a relish tray, or for a crunchy, healthy snack.

Makes 2 pints

½ cup / 120 mL white wine vinegar

¼ cup / 60 mL water

1½ tablespoons kosher salt

1 tablespoon granulated sugar

1½ teaspoons ground coriander

1½ pounds / 680 g carrots, peeled

Few sprigs fresh cilantro

Peel from 1 organic lemon, cut in strips

2 teaspoons coriander seeds, cracked

In a small saucepan, heat the vinegar and water just to a boil to make a brine. Add the salt, sugar, and ground coriander, reduce the heat to low, and stir occasionally until the salt and sugar dissolve, about 3 minutes. Remove from the heat and set aside.

Trim the carrots and cut them into 5-inch / 13 cm sticks about ¼ inch / .5 cm thick. Pack the carrots tightly into 2 pints jars, tucking in the cilantro sprigs and lemon peel as you go, and top with the cracked coriander seeds.

Ladle the brine into the packed jars, leaving ½-inch / 1.5 cm headspace. Cover with the lids and refrigerate. The carrots will gain more flavor each day, but will taste great within a day or two. They'll be crunchy and stay good refrigerated for at least a month.

Mixed Pickle Jar

Mixing vegetables in one jar is a great way to make use of a variety of vegetables you may have on hand, and they look just great in the jar. The tops of the peppers sliced off and placed strategically to face out from the jar look like little flowers—so pretty that you hardly want to disrupt the jar to pull out the pickles to eat!

Makes 1 quart / 1 L

- 2 cups / 475 mL vinegar (apple cider, distilled white, or white wine)
- 1 cup / 240 mL water
- 1 cup / 200 g granulated sugar
- 2 tablespoons kosher salt
- 1 tablespoon each of black peppercorns, mustard seeds, celery seeds, and coriander seeds
- 1 teaspoon red pepper flakes (optional)
- 2 pounds / 900 g vegetables such as carrots, Persian or pickling cucumbers, small multi-colored peppers, cauliflower, and green beans
- 4 garlic cloves, peeled
- Few sprigs fresh dill

In a small saucepan, make a brine by bringing the vinegar, water, sugar, salt, black peppercorns, mustard seeds, celery seeds, coriander seeds, and red pepper flakes (if using) to a boil. Reduce the heat and simmer for 10 minutes, and then remove the pan from the heat and set aside.

Cut the carrots, cucumbers, peppers, and cauliflower into 1-inch / 2.5 cm chunks, slicing the carrots and cucumbers on an angle. Save the tops of the peppers; they look lovely facing out here and there in the jar. Trim the green beans and leave them whole.

Place the cucumbers in a colander in the sink with 2 cups of ice cubes for 30 minutes; this enhances their crunch.

Pack 2 pint jars or 1 quart / 1 L jar tightly with the vegetables, garlic cloves, and dill. Ladle the brine into the jars to cover the vegetables, with ½-inch / 1.5 cm headspace. Cover the jars with their lids and refrigerate.

The pickles are ready to eat as soon as the next day, but gain flavor over time. They'll keep in the refrigerator for a couple of weeks.

Cauliflower Pepper Pickle

I'm always looking for new and flavorful ways to prepare my cauliflower, so I was intrigued when I discovered that the Lebanese often pickle theirs. While raw cauliflower can be a less attractive option on a vegetable platter, pickled it becomes quite the opposite: a real treat.

Makes 3 pints / 1.5 L

1 (2-pound / 900 g) head cauliflower

1 sweet red bell pepper

2½ teaspoons kosher salt, divided

¼ cup / 60 mL white wine vinegar

2 cups / 475 mL neutral oil, such as safflower or canola

Few grinds of black pepper

1½ teaspoons marjoram

¼ teaspoon granulated garlic powder

Core the cauliflower and cut or break it apart into 1- to 2-inch / 2.5 to 5 cm florets.

Core and trim the red pepper and slice it into thin shards, about 2 inches / 5 cm long and ¼ inch / .5 cm thick.

In a 3- or 4-quart / 3 or 4 L pot, blanch the cauliflower by covering it with water by 2 inches / 5 cm and adding 2 teaspoons of the salt. Bring to a boil, reduce the heat to medium, and simmer the cauliflower for 5 minutes. Drain it completely.

In a medium bowl, make a vinaigrette by whisking the remaining ½ teaspoon of salt, vinegar, oil, pepper, marjoram, and garlic powder until the mixture is emulsified.

Pack the cauliflower and red pepper slices into 3 clean pint jars. Ladle the vinaigrette into the packed jars, leaving ½-inch / 1.5 cm headspace. Cover with the lids and refrigerate for a few days to let the flavors meld before enjoying. Store the pickles in the refrigerator for several weeks.

Spiced White Grapes

Spiced grapes are such a unique and delicious addition to the plate. They're wonderful with a cheese platter and charcuterie, as well as a condiment with meats like pork, duck, lamb, and chicken. They also elevate a bowl of yogurt or good vanilla ice cream.

Makes 1 pint / 500 mL

½ cup / 120 mL white wine vinegar

1½ cups / 300 g granulated sugar

1 teaspoon green cardamom pods

½ teaspoon grated nutmeg

½ teaspoon ground ginger

¼ teaspoon kosher salt

1 cinnamon stick

½ teaspoon dried basil

1½ pounds / 680 g seedless white grapes, at room temperature

In a 2-quart / 2 L saucepan, bring everything except the grapes to a boil over medium heat. Reduce the heat to low and simmer for 5 minutes, and then set it aside to cool slightly while slicing the grapes. The mixture is very thick and seems like it's not enough for all of the grapes, but not to worry.

Slice the grapes in half lengthwise. Add them to the spiced syrup and place it over low heat. The sugar may crystallize a bit at this point. Reheat the mixture over medium heat, stirring occasionally, for about 3 minutes, or until the syrup is liquid and the grapes are completely coated. Cool the mixture for 15 minutes.

Spoon the grape mixture into a clean pint / 500 mL jar, including the cinnamon stick and cardamom. Ladle the syrup over them, leaving ½-inch / 1.5 cm headspace. Cover and refrigerate the grapes for 2 days to develop the flavors. Store the grapes in the refrigerator for several weeks.

Fig and Anise Jam with Walnuts

Everyone I've witnessed taste this jam for the first time goes more than a little wild over it. Fig jam makes an unusual, special element on a cheese plate. It is also excellent on toast, or scooped up with flatbread. My mother heads to her fig jam mid-afternoon—a big spoonful straight from the jar.

Makes 1 quart / 1 L

1½ cups / 300 g granulated sugar

¾ cup / 180 mL water

Juice of 1 lemon

1 pound / 450 g dried figs, coarsely chopped (4 cups)

2 cups / 300 g chopped walnuts, toasted

3 tablespoons anise seed

In a 2-quart / 2 L saucepan, combine the sugar, water, and lemon juice. Bring to a boil over high heat, reduce the heat to medium-low, and cook until slightly syrupy, about 5 minutes.

Add the figs, increase the heat to bring the mixture to a boil, and then reduce the heat to medium-low. Simmer, stirring occasionally, until some of the figs break down and the mixture is thickened, about 5 minutes.

Remove the pan from the heat and stir in the chopped nuts and anise seed. Cool the jam for 30 minutes. Spoon it into a quart / 1 L jar, and keep the jam covered with an airtight lid. Store the jam in the refrigerator for several months. Bring to room temperature to soften a bit before serving.

Preserved Watermelon Rind

It's a good thing that sweet watermelon rind preserve is so delicious, because it takes a lot of time to prepare. The steps aren't difficult, but the thick rind requires plenty of soak time—so begin three days in advance. For your generosity of time and patience, you'll be richly rewarded with one of the most surprisingly good sweet pickles you can make or eat. My experience with these pickles is from one place and one place only: the historic Dam Site Inn in Northern Michigan. To walk in is to step back into 1950's "gracious dining," and also to fight the crowds in the summer when everyone is looking for a good fried chicken dinner. Even better than the chicken is the relish platter with removable steel bowls of relishes of every sort, including pickled watermelon rind. I was never so surprised as when I found the preserves in one of my old Lebanese cookbooks—but I shouldn't have been, knowing what a strong tradition the Lebanese have for preserving everything in season.

Makes 1 quart / 1 L

1 (3-pound / 1.35 kg) organic watermelon

3 tablespoons kosher salt

2½ cups / 500 g granulated sugar

1 cup / 240 mL distilled white vinegar

1 cinnamon stick

3 cloves

½ organic lemon, thinly sliced, seeds removed

Cut the watermelon into pieces and cut the rind off of the pink flesh. Peel the green outer skin from the watermelon rind. Cut the rind into 2-inch / 5 cm pieces.

In a large bowl, add the rind with enough water to cover it by a couple of inches / 5 cm, and stir in the salt. Set aside to soak for 8 hours or overnight.

Drain and rinse the rind. Place it in a 4-quart / 4 L saucepan with enough water to cover the rind by a couple of inches / 5 cm. Bring this to a boil and cook over medium-high heat until the rind is tender, no more than 15 minutes. Drain the rind in a colander and place it back in the large bowl.

Combine the sugar, vinegar, cinnamon, and cloves in the pot, along with 2 cups / 475 mL of water. Bring the mixture to a boil for 5 minutes. Pour the syrup over the watermelon and stir in the lemon slices. Refrigerate for 8 hours, or overnight.

Back in the 4-quart / 4 L saucepan, heat the watermelon rind in its syrup over high heat to boiling; reduce the heat to medium-high and boil until the rind is translucent, about 40 minutes. Pack the hot watermelon pickles loosely into a clean quart / 1 L jar. Ladle the hot syrup (including the cinnamon stick, cloves, and lemon) into the packed jar, leaving ½-inch / 1.5 cm headspace. Wipe the rim of the jar with a damp paper towel and top the jar with the lid. The rind can be eaten immediately. Store in the refrigerator for several weeks.

Apricot Preserves

Mish-mish, or apricot, is the darling of all fruits for the Lebanese. These wonderful preserves bring out the ultimate apricot flavor, and are a staple. The preserve's sweet-tart flavor goes outrageously well on a great piece of toast with something creamy, like labneh (page 29), or cream cheese, or ricotta, or . . . you get the picture. I loved watching my 2-year-old godson Cam (named for my father, Camille), when his mom Amara fed him apricot jam on toast for the first time: he couldn't stop saying *More! Ap-cot!*

Makes 2 pints

2 pounds / 900 g fresh ripe apricots

1⅓ cups / 265 g granulated sugar, plus more as needed

¼ cup / 60 mL water

Juice of ½ to 1 lemon

Pit the apricots by splitting them between your thumbs and removing the pit. They give way with ease.

In a heavy medium saucepan, add the sugar and water and stir just to combine. Cook over medium heat until the sugar has melted and the mixture begins to simmer.

Add half of the pitted apricots, increase the heat to medium-high, and bring them to a boil. Reduce the heat to low and simmer, stirring frequently with a wooden spoon, until the apricots are very soft and falling apart, about 30 minutes.

Add the rest of the apricots, increase the heat to medium-high, and bring the mixture back to a boil. Reduce the heat to low and simmer, stirring frequently until the mixture thickens and the apricots have softened but some pieces still remain, another 30 minutes. Taste. Depending on how tart the preserves are, and how tart you like it, add 1 tablespoon or more of lemon juice. If the preserves are too tart, add 1 tablespoon or more of sugar. Cool the preserves for 15 minutes, and then ladle into 2 pint jars. Top the jars with their lids and refrigerate for up to 1 year.

Apricot-Lime Fruit Leather

Homemade fruit leather is easy to make, and a great way to use up an abundance of most any ripe summer fruit. Thick apricot fruit leather is a traditional Lebanese sweet known as *quamerdeen* (pronounced um-ur-DEEN). A Silpat will release the fruit leather with the most ease, but parchment paper can also be used to line the pan. Use this recipe to make leather with all kinds of fruit (such as sweet or tart cherries, grapes, plums, or peaches). Note that the recipe requires a low and slow (6- to 8-hour) baking time.

Makes 8 servings

3 pounds / 1.35 kg pitted, coarsely chopped apricots (about 4 cups)

Juice of 2 limes

¼ cup / 60 mL water

⅓ cup / 80 mL / 65 g agave nectar or granulated sugar

Line a heavy-duty sheet pan with a Silpat or parchment paper. Place one of the oven racks in the middle position, and turn on the oven to 200°F / 95°C.

In a 4-quart / 4 L heavy saucepan, bring the apricots, lime juice, and water to a boil over medium-high heat. The sweetness of your fruit will determine how much sugar to add, so once the fruit begins to break down, add the agave nectar or sugar 1 tablespoon at a time. Taste the mixture after each addition to determine if it is sweet enough. If not, add more.

Reduce the heat to medium-low and simmer for 10 minutes, or until the fruit is entirely broken down and the mixture is sauce-like. Remove the pan from the heat and cool for 10 minutes.

Puree the cooked fruit in a blender or food processor (in batches, depending on capacity) until smooth, about a minute. Tap the bowl of puree on the countertop to release any air bubbles. Pour the puree on the lined sheet pan and spread it with an offset spatula or back of a spoon, leaving an inch / 2.5 cm rim, to about ¼-inch / .5 cm thickness. Be sure to spread the puree evenly; if the edges are too thin, they will become overcooked.

Bake for 6 to 8 hours, or until the leather is mostly dried but still slightly tacky to touch. Peel the leather from the Silpat or parchment, and wrap it with waxed paper or plastic wrap (you can cut the leather in half and wrap the halves separately). To serve, cut or tear the leather into pieces. Store the leather, well-wrapped, at room temperature for several weeks.

Arabic Coffee

Orange Blossom and
Raw Honey Tisane (Café Blanc)

Fresh Mint Tea

Cinnamon Stick Tea

Cardamom Green Tea

Cucumber Spritzer with Mint

Thick Hot Chocolate with Cinnamon

Lebanese Mimosa with Sugar Rim

Strawberry–Rose Lemonade

Sparkling Pomegranate Cocktail
with St. Germain

Arabic Coffee

Arabic coffee, also known as Turkish coffee, is made in small batches on the stovetop in an ibrik, a special pot with a wide bottom and narrow neck; a small saucepan works well too. Any dark roast coffee bean can be used for Arabic coffee, but authentic Arabic coffee can also be found in Middle Eastern groceries. The key either way is that the coffee is ground extremely fine ("Arabic grind"), pulverized to a powder. This strong coffee is like espresso in that it is served in demitasse cups; traditional Arabic coffee cups don't have handles and can be found inexpensively in sets.

Makes 4 servings

2 cups / 475 mL cold water

2 tablespoons finely ground Arabic coffee

1 teaspoon granulated sugar (optional)

1 green cardamom pod (optional)

Place the cold water in an ibrik or small saucepan and stir in the coffee, along with the sugar and cardamom, if using. The coffee need not be completely dissolved at the start; that will happen as it boils.

Bring the coffee to a boil over high heat, stirring occasionally. When it comes just to a boil, remove it from the heat and gently stir so that the coffee doesn't boil over. Return the pot to the heat and bring the coffee back to a boil, still stirring. Remove the coffee from the heat and pour it, along with its foam, into four demitasse or small handle-less Arabic coffee cups. Serve the coffee hot.

Orange Blossom and Raw Honey Tisane
(Café Blanc)

This incredibly simple drink, known as café blanc, has become an obsession of mine, ever since I started avoiding caffeinated or pre-sweetened drinks. It's been my constant companion through long, cold Michigan winters, a total comfort for body and soul. Any honey can be used to make this heavenly elixir, but the flavor of creamed raw honey is especially complex and delicious.

Makes 4 servings

4 cups / 950 mL boiling water

4 teaspoons creamed raw honey, divided among the cups

½ teaspoon orange blossom water, divided among the cups

Pour the boiling water into teacups or mugs. Stir a teaspoon of honey and ⅛ teaspoon of orange blossom water into each cup. Serve hot, or cool to room temperature and serve the tisane cold, over ice.

Fresh Mint Tea

What a great surprise it was when I learned that making fresh herbal tea is as simple as pouring boiling water over muddled herbs. This opened up a whole new way to enjoy the scent and flavor of all kinds of herbs, but most especially our Lebanese favorite, fresh spearmint. Green or black tea can also be added to the pot with the mint leaves.

Makes 4 servings

5 sprigs fresh mint

4 cups / 950 mL boiling water

Granulated sugar or honey, for serving

Remove a handful of the mint leaves from their stems and coarsely chop them. Place the chopped leaves and the sprigs of mint into a warmed teapot.

Pour the boiling water over the mint in the teapot and steep for 5 minutes. Give the tea a stir before pouring it into teacups. Use a strainer when pouring out the tea if you prefer not to have the loose leaves in the tea. Serve the tea with sugar or honey.

Cinnamon Stick Tea

Slowly brewing the cinnamon in the water, and then resting the tea before heating it back up, extracts the most flavor from the cinnamon sticks. To make cinnamon black tea, add the tea leaves or bags to the water after it boils the second time, and steep for 3 minutes.

Makes 4 servings

4 cups / 950 mL water

3 cinnamon sticks, broken in half

Granulated sugar or honey, for serving

In a small saucepan, combine the water and cinnamon sticks. Bring the mixture to a boil slowly over medium heat. Remove the saucepan from the heat and set it aside to steep for 15 minutes longer, when the tea will achieve a rich red color and deeper cinnamon flavor. Reheat the tea to a boil, and then strain the tea into a warm teapot or directly into teacups, and serve immediately with granulated sugar or honey.

Cardamom Green Tea

Green cardamom and green tea make a great pair, with the subtlety of the green tea allowing the distinctive taste of cardamom to shine.

Makes 4 servings

4 cups / 950 mL boiling water

4 teaspoons or 2 bags green tea

12 green cardamom pods, crushed

Granulated sugar or honey, for serving

In a warm teapot, pour the boiling water over the green tea and cardamom pods. Steep for just a minute or two (longer can release bitter tannins). Serve immediately by straining the tea into teacups, with sugar or honey for sweetening.

PORCH TIME

emonade on the front porch is sort of iconic in my world. The first time I met my husband, when I was just 12 years old, I held out an icy glass of pink lemonade to him on our front porch in Harbor Springs. My Strawberry-Rose Lemonade (page 232) was inspired by that pink lemonade day, but also by a rose water drink that my mother and my sister-in-law, Ruth, recalled for me after their trip to Lebanon in the summer of 2006.

It was a memorable trip for lots of reasons, not the least of which was that they were there to meet the newborn baby boy whom my brother and his wife were about to adopt. When they arrived, baby John's caregiver welcomed them with small glasses of rose-scented lemonade. Doesn't that sound lovely? Long-awaited baby—all fingers and toes accounted for—in open arms, tears of joy, refreshing lemonade in hand, and the land of our ancestors experienced by all of them for the first time.

And it *was* lovely, except that the rose water lemonade was . . . what my mom calls "undrinkable." Her sheer force of will, and the unspoken laws that govern respect for another woman's hospitality, got her through half of a glass. It tasted more, much more, like a bottle of perfume than something you'd drink, she said. This bothered me, and stuck with me, because I wanted rose-scented lemonade in Lebanon to taste really good, exotic, unlike any lemonade any of us had ever tasted (okay, at this point in life I'm well aware of my inclination toward the romantic, the dramatic, but don't stop reading here, because what's to follow truly is dramatic, if not romantic).

The trip went from joyous baby-ogling to Middle Eastern war overnight. My brother and mother had left Ruth in Lebanon, where she was to keep baby John with her for a couple of weeks, when my brother would return to finalize the adoption. Instead, she found herself sweating it out for hours on a Beirut beach in 110-degree heat with a newborn in her arms, waiting to board a U.S. military boat taking American citizens there out of harm's way, to Cyprus. And that was considered a whopping success after a week of harrowing attempts to determine how to get Ruth home with a baby that was not yet legally hers. The answer was a "humanitarian visa," secured just hours before the last American boat taking U.S. citizens to safety left harbor.

What happened next is hardly speakable, but it must be said. If there's one thing I've learned in this life, it's that for every joy there is a sorrow. The Lebanese poet Khalil Gibran's "On Joy and Sorrow" sings that the deeper sorrow carves into your being, the more joy you can contain. That we can't have one without the other. That this is what it means to be alive. We have to find some way to accept it, don't we?

Ruth, not long after that war-torn visit to Beirut to adopt her baby, started coughing a lot, and couldn't stop. It might be pneumonia, we wondered. But there was a more awful word spoken, definitively, about a cancer that would soon take her life despite the fact that she was a new mom to a Lebanese baby boy with curly hair

and brown eyes she'd brought out of Lebanon in the middle of a war.

This topic may, I understand, seem heavy for a cookbook, and for what is for many of us our first heart-to-heart conversation, you and me. But some relationships take off quickly when old souls meet, and matters of the heart just seem to fall out on the table.

Plus, this lemonade is special. This lemonade is about hope. It's about the hope Ruth had for her life, and the hope that her children and my brother gave her. It's about wishing such a deep sorrow never had to be carved into any of our beings, but grateful for the joy that would fill the jagged etchings left behind. It's about wanting that original rose water that welcomed my family to Lebanon to taste as perfect as that moment seemed.

Now, when summer blooms Up North in Michigan, I make my best, most delicious rosy strawberry lemonade for the family and our treasure, John, and take it to the front porch to share a glass with them there.

Strawberry-Rose Lemonade

Lemonade infused with red fruit takes it to another level of lovely. In spring, I use strawberries, and in mid-summer, raspberries and tart cherries (strain the cooked fruit before adding either to the lemonade).

Makes 8 servings

3 cups / 600 g granulated sugar, divided

8 cups / 2 L water, or as needed, divided

Juice from 8 large lemons, strained

4 cups / 600 g strawberries, hulled and coarsely chopped, with 4 whole berries reserved for serving

1 teaspoon rose water

Combine 2 cups / 400 g of the sugar and 2 cups / 475 mL of the water in a medium saucepan and bring them to a boil over medium-high heat. (Chill the remaining 6 cups / 1.5 L of water.) Once the liquid reaches a boil, reduce the heat and simmer until the sugar is completely dissolved, about 3 minutes. Remove from the heat and stir in the strained lemon juice. Set the syrup aside to cool.

In a small saucepan over medium heat, combine the chopped strawberries and the remaining cup / 200 g of sugar. Bring the mixture to a boil, and then reduce the heat to low and simmer for 3 to 5 minutes, until the berries are very juicy. Use a metal spoon or a potato masher to mash and break up the berries. Stir in the teaspoon of rose water.

Strain the liquid from the strawberries into a small bowl or measuring cup, pressing on the solids to extract as much juice as possible. Set aside the berries for another use (atop vanilla ice cream or yogurt will do just fine . . .).

In a 32-ounce pitcher, mix the lemon syrup and the strawberry-rose syrup. Fill the pitcher with 4 cups / 950 mL of ice-cold water, and stir well. Taste. If the lemonade is too sweet for you, add another cup or 2 / 240 to 475 mL of cold water. If it's not tart enough, add more lemon juice. If you'd like to taste more rose in your lemonade, add another drop or two of rose water.

Fill tall glasses with ice and the lemonade. Cut the remaining whole berries in half, top each glass with a berry half, and serve immediately.

Sparkling Pomegranate Cocktail with St. Germain

My sister Peg is the family mixologist, and she declared St. Germain the "next big thing" years before it was so widely known. She considers herself the progenitor of all drinks St. Germain, and she mixes it into delicious concoctions whenever we all get together. Made from elderflowers, the floral flavor and scent of St. Germain gives it a headiness that feels like a member of the same family as our beloved rose water and orange blossoms.

Serves a crowd

1 part chilled pomegranate juice

1 part chilled prosecco, cava, or other sparkling wine

1 part chilled soda water

Splash of St. Germain for each serving

Mix everything in a pitcher or individual glasses with ice, and serve immediately.

Cucumber Spritzer with Mint

My brother Tom has what can only be described as an unquenchable thirst. He is always looking for something lemony and refreshing to drink, so I thought of him when I created this, in hopes that it would quench his thirst. The cucumber syrup, which is a lovely shade of green and has a summery melon-like flavor, can be made several days in advance and stored in an airtight container in the refrigerator. A splash of gin or vodka and a big squeeze of lemon juice makes this a satisfying cocktail, one Tom approves of wholeheartedly.

Makes 8 servings

1 cup / 240 mL water

1 cup / 200 g granulated sugar

1 (2-inch / 5 cm) piece fresh ginger, peeled and sliced in ¼-inch / .5 cm coins

5 sprigs fresh mint

3 Persian cucumbers, 2 grated (about 1 cup) and 1 thinly sliced

1 (2-liter) bottle chilled soda water

Juice of 1 lemon

In a small saucepan, combine the water, sugar, ginger, and 10 leaves of the mint, torn or chopped into small pieces. Bring the mixture to a boil, and then reduce the heat to medium and simmer for 2 minutes. Remove the syrup from the heat and stir in the grated cucumber. Place the lid on the pot and steep for 30 minutes. Strain the syrup through a fine mesh sieve and set it aside to cool completely.

To make the spritzer in a pitcher, ideally a glass pitcher so the beautiful spritzer is visible, muddle a few mint leaves in a 3-quart / 3 L pitcher. Add the simple syrup, 3 to 4 cups / 700 to 950 mL of ice cubes, a few cucumber slices, the soda water, and the lemon juice. Fill 8 tall glasses with ice cubes, cucumber slices, and mint leaves. Pour the spritzer into each glass and serve immediately.

To make the spritzer in individual glasses, muddle a few mint leaves in the bottom of each glass. Pour a couple of tablespoons of the cucumber syrup into each, and then add ice, a few cucumber slices, and a couple of mint leaves. Pour the soda water into the glasses with a squeeze of lemon juice; stir and serve immediately.

Thick Hot Chocolate with Cinnamon

Hot cocoa has its place in the world, but thick drinking chocolate? That belongs on our unforgettable lists. When I was served this hot chocolate in Spain, it was nothing like any hot chocolate I'd ever tasted, with its excellent custard-like texture and warm cinnamon spice note. Once I understood how they made it, it's been my special treat, especially for my mid-winter birthday around Valentine's Day. Go deep, dark, and high-quality with your chocolate, and serve the hot chocolate in small cups.

Makes 4 servings

2 cups / 475 mL milk (whole or 2 percent; if using skim, increase the cornstarch by 1 teaspoon), divided

1 tablespoon cornstarch

¼ teaspoon ground cinnamon

3 to 4 ounces / 85 to 115 g highest quality chocolate, 60 to 70 percent cacao, finely chopped

In a small bowl, stir ¼ cup / 60 mL of the milk slowly into the cornstarch until it is dissolved.

In a small saucepan, pour the cornstarch slurry into the remaining milk and stir in the cinnamon. Bring the mixture just to a boil over medium heat, stirring constantly.

Reduce the heat to medium-low and add the chocolate, continuing to stir until the chocolate melts and the milk is slightly thickened (it will lightly coat the back of a wooden spoon).

Pour the chocolate into little cups, and serve immediately.

Lebanese Mimosa with Sugar Rim

Anything that gives me a "sugar rim" tells me it's time to celebrate. These mimosas are elevated with orange blossom water, perfect for toasting a special day.

Serves a crowd

Turbinado sugar, for rims

1 part chilled fresh-squeezed or best quality orange juice

1 part chilled prosecco, cava, or other sparkling wine

2 drops orange blossom water for each serving

2 dashes small-batch orange bitters (such as Fee Brothers) for each serving

Wet the rims of champagne coupes or flutes by dipping the edges in a small bowl of cold water. Place the turbinado sugar in a small bowl and dip the rim of each glass in the sugar.

Mix the mimosas in a pitcher, pour them into the sugar-rimmed coupes or flutes, and serve immediately.

FRESH AND CLASSIC LEBANESE MENUS

A Summer Cookout

Pita Chips with Baba Gannouj
pages 37 & 68

Yogurt-Marinated Chicken Skewers
with Toum Garlic Sauce
page 123

Spiced Lamb Kofta Burgers
page 113

Warm Potato Salad with Lemon and Mint
page 75

Avocado Tabbouleh in Little Gems
page 77

Crunchy Fennel Salad
page 85

Mixed Pickle Jar
page 212

Graham Cracker Ice Cream Sandwiches
made with Mandarin Orange Frozen Yogurt
page 172

Strawberry-Rose Lemonade
page 232

An Elegant Dinner

Phyllo Galette of Labneh,
Caramelized Cherry Tomatoes,
and Kalamata Olives
page 56

Garlic Mushroom Pickles
with Talami Sesame Loaves
pages 210 & 186

Butter Lettuce with
Walnut Vinaigrette
page 73

Pistachio-Crusted Whitefish
with Parsley-Lemon Butter
page 133

Freekeh with Tomato and Chickpeas
page 141

Simply steamed haricot verts
with Toum
page 30

Sticky Date Cake with
Warm Orange Blossom-Caramel Sauce
page 154

Arabic Coffee
page 224

A Spring Luncheon

Cucumber Spritzers with Mint
page 235

Spinach Pies
page 198

Crudité and Labneh Dip with Crushed Red
Pepper and Mint
page 51

Poached White Asparagus with Lemon and
Pistachio Oil
page 58

Hushweh
(Chicken Rice Pilaf with
Butter Toasted Almonds)
page 124

Carrot Coriander Pickle
page 211

Rose Water Meringues
with Roasted Rhubarb
page 150

Graybeh
(Shortbread Cookies)
page 164

A Cocktail Party

Sparkling Pomegranate Cocktail
with St. Germain
page 233

Za'atar Roasted Tomato Crostini
with Labneh
page 52

Ba'albek Sfeha
(Open-Faced Lamb Pies)
page 201

Grape Leaves
with Lemon
page 90

Warm Dates
with Almonds and Lime Zest
page 60

Whipped Hummus with
Crudité and Pita Chips
pages 49 & 37

Array of Cheeses with
Fig and Anise Jam with Walnuts
page 216

Charcuterie Plate
with Spiced White Grapes
page 215

Fresh and Classic Lebanese Menus

A Holiday Brunch

Lebanese Mimosa with Sugar Rim
page 237

Fresh Mint Tea
page 226

Baked Eggs
with Spinach, Labneh, and Sumac
page 128

Tomato and Sweet Onion Salad
page 83

Platter of sliced cucumber
with kalamata olives, olive oil drizzle

Toast made with Talami Sesame Loaves
page 186

Apricot Preserves
page 218

Labneh with Orange, Avocado,
Pomegranate, and Honey
page 181

Sugared Anise Donuts
page 178

Stone Fruit with
Flower Waters and Shaved Coconut
page 183

A Winter Gathering

Mahogany Eggplant
with Labneh and Pomegranate
page 65

Green Bean and Lamb Stew
page 117

Lebanese Vermicelli Rice
page 147

Baked Kibbeh Sahnieh
page 104

Bowl of olives with a plate of Labneh,
olive oil drizzle
page 29

Maryalice's Big Romaine Salad
page 80

Lift
(Hot Pink Turnip Pickle)
page 206

Homemade Pita Bread
page 192

Walnut Baklawa Diamonds
page 158

Cardamom Green Tea
page 229

A Vegan Menu

Pita Chips with Muhammara
(Roasted Red Bell Pepper–Walnut Dip)
pages 37 & 70

Za'atar Kale Chips
page 67

Mujadara with Crispy Onions
page 139

Vegan Tomato Kibbeh
page 108

Fattoush Salad
page 84

Cauliflower Pepper Pickle
page 214

Salted Pistachio Bark with Dried Apricots
(using dairy-free dark chocolate)
page 170

Orange Blossom and Raw Honey Tisane
(Café Blanc)
page 225

A Gluten-Free Menu

Garlicky Lentil Soup with
Swiss Chard and Lemon
page 136

Fresh Herb Falafel
with Tahini-Yogurt Sauce
page 142

Eggplant with
Lamb, Tomato, and Pine Nuts
page 98

Crunchy Fennel Salad
page 85

Pickle Dish of Lift
(Hot Pink Turnip Pickle) and
Carrot Coriander Pickle
pages 206 & 211

Rice Pudding with
Dried Cherries and Pistachios
page 160

Cinnamon Stick Tea
page 228

WHERE TO BUY THE SPECIAL INGREDIENTS AND TOOLS IN THIS BOOK

Every ingredient matters when we're cooking recipes of any kind. I'm always on the hunt for the best (which isn't always the most expensive or rare) ingredients for my Lebanese recipes. Many of the fruits of that quest are now available to you online at the Rose Water & Orange Blossoms shop at maureenabood.com. It's my great pleasure to offer you my special selection of ingredients and tools for your pantry there, including dry skinned chickpeas, dry skinned fava beans, bulgur wheat, lentils, sumac, cinnamon (ground and sticks), fancy California dried apricots, flower waters, mahleb, wooden mah'moul and ka'ik molds, koosa corers, and much more. The products I offer you are the same ones I use on a daily basis in my kitchen. My goal is to make your experience cooking Lebanese recipes as easy, delicious, and rewarding as possible. Here are some additional resources where you can find ingredients and tools.

American Spoon: www.spoon.com
Lebanese-American entrepreneur Justin Rashid founded this northern Michigan treasure, which sells exceptional preserves, dried cherries, and much more from our great state.

Bob's Red Mill: www.bobsredmill.com
For freekeh, as well as the skinned, large white fava beans called for in homemade falafel.

Buy Lebanese: www.buylebanese.com
Offers worldwide delivery of Lebanese specialty items, direct from Lebanon.

Cherry Republic: www.cherryrepublic.com
Order Michigan dried cherries in all sorts of iterations from this special shop in Michigan.

Dayna's Market: www.daynasmarket.com
For imported Lebanese ingredients and tools like vegetable corers (also known as picks) for koosa.

Kalustyan's: www.kalustyans.com.
One of the most extensive offerings of Middle Eastern ingredients, including za'atar, bulgur, flower waters, pomegranate molasses, kataifi and phyllo dough, and much more.

Mymouné: www.mymoune.com
For beautiful imported Lebanese organic flower waters and preserves.

Olive Harvest: www.oliveharvest.com
For authentic, special Lebanese olive oils straight from northern Lebanese soil.

Parthenon Foods: www.parthenonfoods.com
Order your kataifi dough for knafeh online here.

Penzeys: www.penzeys.com
An extensive array of quality spices. Their imported mahleb is excellent.

Pressmeister Oils: www.pressmeister-oils.com
Excellent artisanal nut oils from northern Michigan.

The Spice House: www.thespicehouse.com
Wonderful spices and a very special shop to visit in Chicago.

La Tourangelle: www.latourangelle.com
Exceptional nut oils can be found here.

Yasmeen Bakery: www.yasmeenbakery.com and www.eyasmeen.com
Pita bread is wonderful homemade (page 192), but I would love for you to experience the kind of thin, golden, chewy Lebanese pita that is found only in our professional bakeries and that is such a special part of most every bite we take. Order this wonderful bread online if you don't have a bakery near you and store it in your freezer, where it keeps perfectly for many months.

Ziyad: www.ziyad.com
Here you will find the full catalogue of Ziyad Lebanese products, which are widely available at both large grocery stores and neighborhood import markets.

Acknowledgments

In ordinary life we hardly realize that we receive a great deal more than we give, and that it is only with gratitude that life becomes rich.   —Dietrich Bonhoeffer

There is so much that I have been given, by so many, that has made this book and what I do possible—a great deal more than I could ever give in return. My gratitude knows no bounds.

To my dear agent, Jenni Ferrari-Adler at Union Literary: thank you for partnering with me on the path of this book and showing me the way.

To my talented editor, Kristen Green Wiewora at Running Press, who saw a book in my blog from the get-go: thank you for your remarkable wisdom, insights, and smarts; thank you for never missing a beat, even as you welcomed your new baby mid-project; and thank you for loving this book as much as I do!

To all of the creative people who made this book so beautiful, thank you! Jason Varney, Josh McDonnell, Katie Hatz, Paige Hicks, Chris Lanier, Anna Hampton, and Jennifer Kasius: I'm so impressed.

To Dianne Jacob, Andrea Lynn, Tara Mataraza Desmond, Cheryl Sternman Rule, Kathleen Flinn, Geralyn Lasher, Rebecca Lien, Cindy Hunter Morgan, John and Nicole Osmer, Michael O'Leary, Kathryn Horning and many others who assisted and encouraged me in the development of my proposal and plans.

To the wonderful cooks who gave their time and care testing the recipes for this book, including Kamell Abdnour, Amara Abood, Cathy Abood, Jim Abood, Maria Abood, Maryalice Abood, Pat Abood, Peggy Abood, Dick Abood, Sarah Abood, Sheila Abood, Lynda Balslev, Margy Barile, Teresa Brantley, Katie Capaldi, Barbara Davidge, Katie Dyos, Janet Helm (the pomegranate molasses in a classic fattoush, thank you!), Brian Huggler, Henna Idris, Gabrielle Johnson, the incredible Zoe Komaransky, Geralyn Lasher, Virginia Lasher, Rebecca Lien, Shalini Lobo, Megan Mattingly, Vanita Mirchandani, Janet Moore, Carlos Sandino, the amazing Rosemary Schwendler, Cheryl Spinazze, Cynthia Spivey, Celine Terranova, Rebecca Votto, and Paul Zeidan: wow, you people are so generous! Thank you a million thanks for your time, feedback, and enthusiasm. I learned a great deal from you, and this book has benefitted greatly from your work.

To Fawaz and Awatef Fawaz, thank you for the special visits in your Lebanese kitchen as I wrote this book. Your hospitality, food, and stories always captivate.

To Abouna Vince Farhat: you treated me to one of the finest Lebanese meals I've eaten while describing your family's prized talami recipe, with hand motions included. I can't thank you enough!

To Antonia Allegra, the godmother of all who have dreams of writing about food: I'm so grateful for the faith you have had in me and my writing from the moment we met long ago, and for the help you have given to me all the way here.

To "Tante Marie" Mary Risley and Frances Wilson: your culinary program gave me so many tools, and so much fun, in preparation for writing my blog and this book.

To Ellen Markus, who walked with me through the most fragile and important period of my life toward all that would make my work and this book possible: thank you for lovingly helping me to dive deep and swim far.

To all of my aunts and uncles, Abood and Abowd: the stories you share connect me and everyone in my generation to our precious family history. Thank you for holding your memories close and treasuring them for us.

To my Abood cousins: thank you for coming together to bake and laugh and eat and bake some more for our annual bake-off. I always learn from those gatherings, and the memories we make are golden.

To Aunt Louise: your table overflows with family, wonderful Lebanese food, and joy. Thank you for welcoming me there and for never hesitating to pull out your recipes to share, discuss, and cook with me.

To the readers of the Rose Water & Orange Blossoms blog: your love of Lebanese cuisine, and the stories and photos that bring it to life, has made this book possible. I am deeply grateful for your presence and your friendship.

To my dear family—Michael, Steven, Tom, Amara, Cam, Chris, John, Peggy, Dick, Silvia, Maria, Ricky, Tommy, and Victoria: my gratitude for the love, encouragement, and ongoing cheerleading each one you has given me so kindly and generously. Tom, thank you for believing with your heart (and your wallet!) in my desire to go to culinary school and write this book. Chris, thank you for your brilliant brainstorming, and for gently taste-testing recipes with John. Dick, you are a tremendous cook with a perfect palate, and you always feed me information, ideas, and laughter I can't live without! Peggy, my soul sister, words can't express my gratitude for all you've done to help bring this book to fruition, not the least of which was converting all of the measurements here to the metric system. I hug you and I thank you! My nieces and nephews, you are my pure sunshine, always.

To my mother, Maryalice: You are grace, warmth, and hospitality personified. This book is ours together. Thank you for allowing me to return to your kitchen full-time, and under your wing, to start my life anew to write my blog and this book.

To Dan: you've been the ultimate support and friend (and fatayar taster!) as this book has come into being. Thank you for keeping me laughing and on track. Thank you for being such a *hanoun*—a pure heart—and my husband. I love and adore you.

Index

Page numbers in *italics* indicate photographs.